THE WORLD'S AIRLINERS

UNIFORM WITH THIS BOOK

JOAN BRADBROOKE *The World's Helicopters*

H. F. KING *The World's Fighters*

H. F. KING *The World's Bombers*

H. F. KING *The World's Strike Aircraft*

JOHN STROUD *The World's Civil Marine Aircraft*

JOHN STROUD *The World's Airports*

OLIVER TAPPER *The World's Great Pioneer Flights*

PUTNAM WORLD AERONAUTICAL LIBRARY

THE WORLD'S
AIRLINERS

JOHN STROUD

THE BODLEY HEAD

LONDON SYDNEY TORONTO

© John Stroud 1971
ISBN 0 370 10808 6
Printed and bound in Great Britain for
The Bodley Head
9 Bow Street, London WC2E 7AL
by Cox & Wyman Ltd, Fakenham
Set in Monophoto Baskerville
First published 1971
Revised edition 1975

CONTENTS

ACKNOWLEDGMENTS

The photographs appearing in this book were kindly supplied by AB Aerotransport (page 25); Air France (38); Airspeed (73); BEA (86); BOAC (103); Boeing Company (96, 98); British Aircraft Corporation (120); Bristol Siddeley (42); ČSA (115); de Havilland Aircraft Company (93); Deutsche Lufthansa (8, 29, 36); Fiat (52); Finnair (83); *Flight International* (10, 17, 19, 20, 68); Focke-Wulf (39); Ford Motor Company (56); KLM (33, 45); Lockheed (80, 90, 123); McDonnell Douglas (100, 122); Pierre Regout (12); Sabena (31); Swissair (23, 88); TWA (63); United Air Lines (77); Gordon S. Williams (61, 113).

INTRODUCTION

The word airliner is ignored by most dictionaries but one at least does define it as a large passenger aircraft. However, in aviation the term large is a constantly changing definition as aircraft grow in size. In the mid-1920s a ten/fourteen-seat aeroplane with a span of about 70 ft, a total of 700 hp and a weight of about 12,000 lb was frequently referred to as a giant airliner whereas today an aeroplane of these dimensions, weight and power would be classed as a feederliner. Because the same aircraft can be equally well used for passengers or cargo it is obvious that the term airliner must under some circumstances include cargo aircraft.

Aeroplanes have been operating passenger, mail and cargo services for a little over half a century and many hundreds of individual types of aircraft have been used for these purposes. They have operated throughout the world but their design and production has mainly been confined to the industrial countries of Europe, the United States and Canada, the Soviet Union, and Japan, with limited manufacture in Australia, India and South America.

This book traces the development of the airliner or transport aeroplane from its pioneer days up to the present when the annual total of world air passengers is counted in hundreds of millions. With the very large number of aircraft types involved it has only been possible to describe in any detail the more important aircraft, but for completeness as many others as possible have been mentioned where appropriate.

Flying-boats and, to a lesser extent, seaplanes have played a major part in the development of air transport but unfortunately lack of space prevents their inclusion in this work.

At the end of each chapter there is a table giving the main particulars of the most important types. Because there were many variations on basic types of aircraft, because different engines were fitted and aircraft weights changed during their working lives, these figures must be regarded only as typical for the type.

1

Converted Bombers

During the 1914–18 war the aeroplane developed from a fair-weather low-powered and rather frail flying machine into a reasonably reliable vehicle capable of operation under a wide range of weather conditions, although its working life was generally short and its cost of operation high.

By the end of the war regular commercial air services were seen to be a possibility, but even earlier, in October 1916, George Holt Thomas had founded Aircraft Transport and Travel as the first British airline, although he had to wait until after the war before operations could begin.

After the Armistice the Royal Air Force had the task of flying Government passengers and mail between London and Paris in connection with the Peace Conference, and for this work single-engined de Havilland 4 day bombers and the much bigger twin-engined Handley Page O/400 night bombers were modified for passenger carriage.

The D.H.4 was an equal-span biplane powered by a 360 hp Rolls-Royce Eagle water-cooled engine and had two open cockpits. For passenger carriage it was known as the D.H.4A, and the gunner's cockpit was modified to have two seats which were protected from the weather by a hinged cabin top in which there were windows.

The Handley Page was a big biplane with overhanging top wing, biplane tail, two Eagle engines and four-wheel undercarriage. For passenger use all military equipment was removed and it was given a furnished cabin.

Cross-Channel commercial air services between England and France were begun by Aircraft Transport and Travel on 25 August 1919, when a regular

◀ An A.E.G. G V twin-engined bomber converted for passenger service with Deutsche Luft-Reederei.

The de Havilland 4A used by S. Instone and Co, later Instone Air Line, seen at Hounslow
in February 1920.

London–Paris passenger and goods service was started. D.H.4As and D.H.16s were used, the latter being a four-passenger cabin conversion of the single-engined D.H.9 day bomber.

The second British airline to work cross-Channel services was Handley Page Transport, which began flying London–Paris services on 2 September 1919, with a fleet of O/400 type aircraft. There were

One of the Handley Page O/400s used on early British air services. This aircraft, seen with mixed civil and military markings, carried passengers from London to Manchester on 1 May 1919 – the first day of civil flying in Britain after the 1914–18 war.

several versions of the civil O/400 but they differed only in interior layout and fuel systems. One version, the O/11, was mainly used for cargo. Two of the passenger seats in the Handley Pages were in an open cockpit in the nose and these provided a wonderful view in summer but were freezingly cold in winter and very unpleasant in rain, hail and snow. The O/400s were much more comfortable than the D.H.4As and D.H.16s but were very slow and often took more than four hours to fly the just over 200 miles from London to Paris.

Another British twin-engined bomber which played a part in developing air transport was the Vickers Vimy, which had appeared too late to see active service. Alcock and Brown made the first nonstop transatlantic flight in a Vimy, and Ross Smith, Keith Smith and Sergeants Bennett and Shiers used a Vimy to make the first flight between the United Kingdom and Australia. Both these pioneer long-distance flights were made in 1919 and both aircraft have been preserved, one in the Science Museum in London and the other at Adelaide Airport in South Australia.

Vimy bombers were used by the RAF on the

One of the Farman Line's Renault-engined Farman Goliaths, seen at Brussels in the early 1920s.

Cairo–Baghdad desert air mail service which was opened in June 1921, and developed from the bomber were the Vimy Commercial passenger aeroplane, used by the British Instone Air Line and in China, and the Vernon, Victoria and Valentia bomber-transports for the RAF.

The early French air services were also started with converted wartime aircraft. The best known and most widely used were the single-engined Breguet 14 and the twin-engined Farman Goliath. The Breguet 14 two-seat biplane made its first flight in November 1916 and about 8,000 of them were built; many, with military equipment removed, and in some cases having mail panniers under their lower wings, were used to pioneer the Latécoère Line's mail route through Spain to West Africa as the first stages of the great French air route to South America. Other Breguet 14s were fitted with two-seat cabins (the Breguet 14T) and used on Paris–London and other European services. The most commonly used engine was the water-cooled 300 hp Renault 12Fe which had a big car-type radiator.

The Farman Goliath was for its time one of the most advanced European transport aeroplanes, quite large numbers were built and some remained in service at least until 1933. The Goliath, designed as a bomber, was completed late in 1918 as a passenger aircraft with main cabin for eight passengers and forward cabin for four passengers, all in wicker seats. The pilot's cockpit was open.

As early as March 1919 the Farman Line began flying Goliaths on a Paris–Brussels service and, later, Cie des Grands Express Aériens, Cie des Messageries Aériennes (CMA) and Air Union operated them on Paris–London services. SNETA (Belgium), ČSA (Czechoslovakia) and LARES (Rumania) also used Goliaths. In spite of their ugly appearance, with square-cut wingtips, stalky four-wheel undercarriages and frequently oil-stained cowlings, the Goliaths gave good service and one is known to have flown at least 3,843 hr. There were numerous versions of the Goliath with different engines but most of the airline aircraft had 230 hp or 260 hp Salmson water-cooled radials. Goliaths were almost certainly the first airliners to have their fuselage tops painted white to keep the cabins cool.

The most important pioneer German airline was Deutsche Luft-Reederei which opened its first scheduled service, between Berlin and Weimar, in February 1919. DLR had a wide assortment of aircraft including ex-military A.E.G. J II and L.V.G. C VI single-engined biplanes, and a small number of A.E.G. G V and Friedrichshafen G IIIa twin-engined biplanes.

The L.V.G. C VIs, mostly powered by 200 hp Benz Bz IV engines, carried two passengers or mail or cargo in the open rear cockpit although a few may have been operated with two-seat cabins. The A.E.G. J II was generally similar to the L.V.G., most had the 200 hp Benz, but some, fitted with rather angular two-seat enclosed cabins, were referred to as the A.E.G. K.

The A.E.G. G V and Friedrichshafen G IIIa were quite large biplanes, each powered by two 260 hp Mercedes D.IVa engines and having biplane tails and four-wheel undercarriages. The G IIIa had an enclosed cabin for about six passengers as did some of the G Vs, but most of the big A.E.Gs carried their passengers in a large open cockpit.

The most interesting German wartime aeroplane to be converted for civil operation was the two-seat Junkers-J 10 low-wing monoplane used for flights between Dessau and Weimar. This type was of all-metal construction with corrugated metal skin and led to the design and production of a whole family of Junkers all-metal transport aeroplanes.

All these converted military aeroplanes were capable of flying from small aerodromes, essential for safe operation because engine failures were frequent and forced landings were generally accomplished without serious results. These aircraft were noisy and, to keep reasonably warm, passengers in most of them had to wear flying clothing.

	Span	Length	Passengers	Loaded weight	Cruising speed	Range
de Havilland 16	46′ 5$\frac{7}{8}$″	32′ 0″	4	4,378 lb	100·0 mph	450 miles
Handley Page O/400	100′ 0″	62′ 10$\frac{1}{4}$″	5/14	12,050 lb	70·0 mph	500 miles
Breguet 14	47′ 1$\frac{1}{4}$″	29′ 6″	2	4,374 lb	77·6 mph	285 miles
Farman Goliath	86′ 10″	47′ 0″	12	10,515 lb	74·5 mph	248 miles
A.E.G. J II	44′ 2″	25′ 11″	2	3,571 lb	93·2 mph*	372 miles
L.V.G. C VI	42′ 7$\frac{3}{4}$″	24′ 7″	2	3,086 lb	99·4 mph*	350 miles

* Maximum speed.

2

British Biplanes

Having begun its air services with converted bombers, Britain began to design and build specialised commercial transport aeroplanes. There were numerous types which enjoyed varying degrees of success but only the more important can be described.

There were three main families of these aircraft, those of de Havilland, Handley Page and Vickers, with Shorts building flying-boats.

De Havilland's first civil transport to enter service was the D.H.18 which first flew in March 1920. This was a wood and fabric biplane with a cabin for eight passengers and an open cockpit for the pilot. Six were built, each powered by a 450 hp Napier Lion water-cooled engine, and they were operated by Aircraft Transport and Travel, Instone Air Line, Daimler Airway and Handley Page Transport mostly on cross-Channel routes.

A direct descendant of the D.H.18 was the much improved D.H.34 which entered service in April 1922 with Instone Air Line and Daimler Airway. The new type resembled the D.H.18 but had seats for up to nine passengers, its open cockpit had seats for a crew of two, and the engine used was the 450 hp Napier Lion. The combination of D.H.34 and Lion engine set a number of records for reliability – one record, set in June 1922, was when five single trips were flown in one day over the London–Paris route by one of the Daimler aircraft. D.H.34s were used on services between London and Manchester and from London to Paris, Brussels, Amsterdam, Cologne and Berlin. It is believed that twelve were built including one for the USSR, and seven passed to Imperial Airways when that airline was founded in 1924. The last of them were withdrawn in March 1926 and their engines used in the new fleet of Handley Page W.10s.

A smaller de Havilland transport was the D.H.50 which had a cabin for four passengers, and first flew in July 1923, powered by a 230 hp Siddeley Puma water-cooled engine. The D.H.50s saw little airline service in Britain but played an important part in developing air transport in Australia where some were built by Qantas and West Australian Airways. A number of Australian-built aircraft had Bristol Jupiter air-cooled engines, and at least two remained in service until 1942. A British-built D.H.50 was used by Alan Cobham on outstanding air route survey flights to Cape Town, Rangoon and Australia.

A development of the D.H.50 was the D.H.61 Giant Moth, with accommodation for six passengers. Most were powered by 450/500 hp Bristol Jupiter engines and, like the D.H.50s, did valuable work in Australia and New Guinea. When the Australia–England air mail service started in December 1934, the Qantas D.H.61 *Diana* and a D.H.50 carried the mail over the first stage from Brisbane to Darwin. Three D.H.61s saw service in Canada, one being operated by Western Canada Airways.

Handley Page's first purely civil transport was the twin-engined W.8, completed in 1919. It was a biplane with single fin and rudder and four-wheel main undercarriage, powered by two 450 hp Napier Lion engines and having accommodation for fifteen passengers. The W.8 saw some service on Handley Page Transport's London–Paris route, and led to a series of aircraft of similar layout, the W.8b, W.8e, W.8f, W.9 and W.10.

The W.8b, with two 360 hp Rolls-Royce Eagle engines and seats for fourteen passengers, entered service with Handley Page Transport in May 1922. Four were built in the United Kingdom, three being used by Handley Page Transport and Imperial Airways and one being sold to Belgium where another four were constructed for the Belgian airline Sabena.

The W.8f Hamilton was Imperial Airways' first three-engined airliner. It entered service in November 1924, had one Rolls-Royce Eagle and two Armstrong Siddeley Puma engines, seats for twelve passengers, and was generally similar to the W.8e of which one was built by Handley Page and ten in Belgium.

The W.9 Hampstead was slightly bigger than the W.8 series, had fourteen seats, and three 385 hp Armstrong Siddeley Jaguar air-cooled engines which were later replaced by 420 hp Bristol Jupiters. The sole W.9 served Imperial Airways from 1926, after being named in a ceremony at Croydon along with

Handley Page Transport Handley Page W.8b RMA *Princess Mary* at Croydon in May 1922.
On the left is the W.8b RMA *Prince George*.

four W.10s which were each powered by two 450 hp Napier Lions and had accommodation for sixteen passengers. Two W.10s were lost in the English Channel but the other two worked on European routes for several years and afterwards played a part in the development of inflight refuelling when they served as tankers.

Already mentioned briefly as a development of

the Vickers Vimy bomber was the Vimy Commercial. One of these, the blue and silver *City of London*, used by Instone from the spring of 1920 and then by Imperial Airways from April 1924 until July 1925, was probably the best known of all early British transport aeroplanes. Starting life as a passenger aeroplane with ten seats, it was destined to become one of the first cargo aircraft and, after its retirement, a summer-house. Vimy Commercials were supplied to China and a few flew the first Chinese air services.

Far less successful was Vickers' single-engined passenger- and cargo-carrying Vulcan, known as the Flying Pig. These were eight-passenger aircraft fitted with a Rolls-Royce Eagle or Napier Lion engine, and nine were built. Used by Instone and Imperial Airways, they were designed to provide low-cost operation but proved a failure.

When Imperial Airways was formed in 1924 as the British national airline, it took over the aircraft of the pioneer companies but decided on the policy of only operating multi-engined aircraft on passenger services. Its first new twin- and three-engined aircraft were the direct developments of the Handley Page W.8b, but in 1926 it began taking delivery of a small fleet of much more advanced aircraft. These were the Armstrong Whitworth Argosy biplanes which, although still fabric-covered, had metal structures.

They had three 385 hp Armstrong Siddeley Jaguar air-cooled engines and accommodation for twenty passengers or eighteen if a buffet and a steward were carried. The Argosy was used to open the *Silver Wing* lunch-time service to Paris and, later, worked on part of the England–Africa route.

One of Imperial Airways' main tasks was the establishment of long-distance services linking the United Kingdom with British territories overseas. The first to be planned was the route between England and India and this entailed operating from aerodromes at high altitude and in very high temperatures. For these critical conditions, encountered between Egypt and India, a fleet of de Havilland 66 Hercules biplanes was designed and built. These were large aircraft each fitted with three 420 hp Bristol Jupiter engines and having accommodation for up to eight passengers. One Hercules left Croydon in December 1926 on the first survey flight to India, and in January 1927 they were used to open the first stage of the India route, between Cairo and Baghdad and Basra. In 1929 the Hercules began flying right through to India and in 1932 were used to extend the Africa route from Kenya to Cape Town. Eleven were built, including four used by West Australian Airways to establish air services across the continent from Perth to Adelaide.

Although the Argosy and Hercules did wonderful

Imperial Airways' Armstrong Whitworth Argosy *City of Glasgow* leaving Croydon with the
first India-bound mail, 30 March 1929.

work, it was realised that larger, more reliable and more comfortable aircraft were required. As a result in 1931 Imperial Airways introduced the large four-engined Handley Page 42s. This type was built in two versions, the 38-passenger Heracles class for European service and the 24-passenger Hannibal class for use between Egypt and India and Egypt and Central Africa. They were powered by four 490/555 hp Bristol Jupiter engines, mounted two on the lower wing and two on the upper wing, had

The Handley Page 42 *Hannibal* which entered service with Imperial Airways in June 1931.

metal structures, mostly fabric-covered, and two very comfortably furnished cabins which were like Pullman railway carriages, had galleys, and introduced completely new standards of service to air travel.

Eight H.P.42s were built and each flew more than a million miles, and together they carried more than a million passengers in perfect safety before the start of the 1939–45 war. The main disadvantage of the Hannibal and Heracles biplanes was that their cruising speed was too low for them to compete with the new generation of fast monoplanes.

Before turning completely to monoplanes, Imperial Airways ordered two more types of biplane. One was the Short L.17 – of which there were two, *Scylla* and *Syrinx* – and the other was the de Havilland 86, described later. *Scylla* and *Syrinx* were large four-engined biplanes which were hurriedly-built landplane adaptations of the Short S.17 Kent flying-boats, urgently needed because Imperial Airways had a fleet shortage. These large biplanes mostly worked on the London–Paris and London–Brussels–Cologne routes. The *Syrinx* was at one time used as a mock-up for Short C class flying-boat cabins.

	Span		Length		Passengers	Loaded weight	Cruising speed	Range
de Havilland 18	51′	2$\frac{3}{4}$″	39′	0″	8	7,000 lb	100 mph	400 miles
Vickers Vimy Commercial	68′	1″	42′	8″	10	12,500 lb	84 mph	450 miles
de Havilland 34	51′	0″	39′	0″	9	7,200 lb	105 mph	365 miles
Handley Page W.8b	75′	0″	60′	1″	14	12,000 lb	90 mph	500 miles
Vickers Vulcan	49′	0″	38′	0″	8	6,750 lb	103 mph	430 miles
Handley Page W.10	75′	0″	58′	4″	16	13,780 lb	100 mph	—
Armstrong Whitworth Argosy	90′	0″	65′	0″	18/20	18,000 lb	90 mph	415 miles
de Havilland 66 Hercules	79′	6″	56′	0″	8	15,600 lb	95 mph	400 miles
Handley Page 42	130′	0″	89′	9″	24/38	28,000/ 29,500 lb	100 mph	580 miles

3

The All-metal Junkers

In the pioneering period of air transport most aircraft manufacturing countries persisted with the biplane, generally with wood or metal structure covered with fabric or in some cases partly with plywood. Germany also built transport biplanes but made two major contributions to the development of the transport aeroplane – the design of all-metal structures and the use of the cantilever monoplane, that is an aircraft whose wing has no external bracing.

By far the biggest producer of German transport aircraft was Junkers, and as early as 1909 Professor Hugo Junkers had made drawings of a thick-wing cantilever monoplane. The first Junkers all-metal aeroplane appeared in 1915 and during 1917 there appeared for the first time a Junkers cantilever low-wing monoplane with corrugated metal skin.

As soon as the war ended, Junkers began design of the first all-metal transport monoplane which was destined to be put into production and enter airline service. This was the J 13, soon to be re-designated F 13, and it made its first flight on 25 June 1919.

In layout the F 13 was a single-engined low-wing monoplane with semi-enclosed cockpit for two crew and a completely enclosed cabin for four passengers. Originally the water-cooled engine was a 160/170 hp Mercedes D.IIIa but the early production aeroplanes had the 185 hp BMW IIIa. The F 13 remained in production until 1930, a total of 322 was built, they had a wide variety of engines and there were some sixty to seventy variations on the basic design. F 13s operated on wheel, float and ski undercarriages and played a big part in establishing air transport

One of Ad Astra Aero's Junkers-F 13 twin-float seaplanes.

in Europe and many other parts of the world.

The F 13 led to a whole series of transport aeroplanes all using the same basic layout and structure although they became progressively bigger, heavier and faster as well as more reliable.

· The next most important step by Junkers was production of the G 23 which first flew in 1924. This had nearly double the span and wing area of the original J 13 and was more than double the weight, but most important was the fact that it had three engines and, as far as can be ascertained,

appears to have been the first three-engined all-metal monoplane to enter airline service.

G 23s had seats for nine passengers, and the early version was powered by a 195 hp Junkers-L 2 and two 100 hp Mercedes engines; but the power was insufficient, and to overcome this a variety of engine installations followed. In 1925 the very similar G 24 was produced. There were more than twenty variants of the G 24 and after a series of modifications to the G 23s it was very difficult to distinguish between the types. Deutsche Lufthansa in Germany, AB Aerotransport in Sweden, Aero O/Y in Finland, SHCA in Greece, Syndicato Condor in Brazil, UAE in Spain and a number of other airlines used G 23s and G 24s – some on twin floats.

After a number of years in service, some of Lufthansa's G 24s were modified, as F 24s, to have a shorter-span wing and single engine and it was one of these which became the first Diesel-powered aeroplane to fly in airline service, between Berlin and Amsterdam in 1932.

A much improved three-engined Junkers was the G 31 which entered service with Lufthansa in 1928. This type still retained the low-wing layout and corrugated metal skin but, unlike the earlier types, had twin fins and rudders. There was accommodation for eleven to fifteen passengers in three separate cabins. Although only thirteen of these aircraft are known to have been built there were a number of versions and several types of engines were used – mostly air-cooled radials such as the 450 hp Gnome Rhône Jupiter, the Siemens Jupiter and the 525 hp BMW Hornet.

Four G 31s, with Pratt & Whitney Hornet engines, lengthened noses and large cargo holds (24 ft by 6 ft 5 in by 5 ft 9 in), were used by Guinea Airways and Bulolo Gold Dredging for the carriage of heavy loads across the mountains from the coast of New Guinea to the goldfields. Between April 1931 and March 1932 these G 31s carried 2,500 tons including three complete gold dredgers. That was the first big airfreighting task ever attempted.

More direct successors to the F 13 were the single-engined Junkers-W 33 and W 34. These were designed mainly for cargo work but they undertook a wide range of duties including passenger carriage, and on wheels and floats they worked in many parts of the world. It was one of these, the W 33 *Bremen*, which in April 1928 made the first successful east-to-west aeroplane crossing of the North Atlantic – the flight from Dublin to Greenly Island off Labrador taking 37 hours.

All these Junkers monoplanes, although much in advance of the more widely used biplanes, were of quite orthodox layout, except for the big four-engined G 38 which first flew in November 1929.

As far back as 1909 Hugo Junkers worked on designs for flying-wing transport aeroplanes and envisaged flying-wings carrying from a hundred to a thousand people across the Atlantic in $1\frac{1}{2}$ days, and in 1923 there was the J 1000 project for a 262 ft $5\frac{1}{2}$ in span hundred-passenger transatlantic flying-wing. However, all these designs were over-ambitious and no large Junkers flying-wing was built, but the bat-like G 38 was to some extent a flying-wing although it did have a fuselage and a biplane tail unit.

The G 38's wing had a maximum thickness of 5 ft 7 in and in its centre section it housed two two-seat passenger cabins, the four engines and the fuel tanks. In its final form the G 38 had its cabins on two decks and total accommodation was for 34 passengers and seven crew.

Originally the G 38 was powered by two 400 hp Junkers-L 8 and two 800 hp L 88 engines but later the aircraft had four 750 hp Junkers Jumo 204 heavy-oil (Diesel) engines. All were accessible in flight.

Two G 38s were built but only one was used in regular service although at least six examples of a bomber version were built in Japan.

On 13 October 1930, a large Junkers single-engined cargo monoplane made its first flight. This was the Ju 52 designed by Ernst Zindel. A small

AB Aerotransport (Swedish Air Lines) Junkers-Ju 52/3m *Götaland*.

number was built, they flew with a variety of engines and used both wheel and float undercarriages, but they did not themselves play a major rôle in air transport. However, developed from the Ju 52 was one of the best known of all transport aeroplanes, the three-engined Ju 52/3m which first flew in April 1932.

The Ju 52/3m was the last of the Junkers transports to have an all-corrugated metal skin. Ju 52/3ms were built in many versions with a wide range of engines although most of the civil aircraft had 750/

830 hp BMW 132 air-cooled radials.

The first production Ju 52/3ms were supplied to Lloyd Aereo Boliviano in Bolivia and other early examples went to Lufthansa, Aero O/Y and AB Aerotransport. The Ju 52/3m became the main type used by Lufthansa, it served with a considerable number of European airlines, did useful work in South America, South Africa and China, and became the standard Luftwaffe transport, being used in the invasions of the Low Countries, Scandinavia and Crete. In the United Kingdom British Airways used three Ju 52/3ms for night mail services.

Total production is believed to have been 4,835 of which 170 were built in Spain and more than 400 in France.

After the war French-built Ju 52/3ms were used by a number of French airlines including Air France, some captured aircraft were used on United Kingdom domestic routes by British European Airways, and a few Scandinavian-operated examples were sold for work in New Guinea. Some Ju 52/3ms were still in service with the Swiss Air Force in early 1975.

Standard accommodation was for fifteen to seventeen passengers and the type operated on wheels, twin floats and skis. One example is preserved in the Deutsches Museum in Munich and another in Berlin.

To meet the competition from the Lockheed Orions ordered by Swissair, in 1932 Junkers completed and flew its single-engined Ju 60 which had a two-spar wing with corrugated metal skin but smooth-skinned fuselage. The Ju 60 was used by Lufthansa but the production version was the Ju 160 which incorporated many modifications and dispensed altogether with corrugated skin in favour of smooth sheet.

The Ju 160 first flew in June 1934, had a retractable undercarriage, accommodation for six passengers and was powered by a 660 hp BMW 132E air-cooled radial engine. Lufthansa introduced Ju 160s into service in 1935 and the prototype and about twenty production aircraft operated mainly on German domestic services. One Ju 160 was reported to have been used by Manchuria Airtransport.

The Ju 86, which first flew on 4 November 1934, was a twin-engined passenger and freight aircraft and the first transport design to have Diesel engines. It was not particularly successful with the 600 hp Junkers Jumo 205C heavy-oil engines and as a result a number of different engines were fitted to this type including BMW 132 and Pratt & Whitney Hornet air-cooled radials and, for South Africa, the liquid-cooled Rolls-Royce Kestrel.

In layout the Ju 86 was a low-wing monoplane with 'double-wing' trailing edge ailerons and flaps, twin fins and rudders, retractable undercarriage and smooth all-metal skin. The oval-section fuselage was very slender and this gave a very cramped passenger cabin in which there were ten seats.

Lufthansa employed about fifteen Ju 86s, South African Airways had eighteen, Swissair two, Swedish Air Lines one (used for mail services), two were supplied to Lloyd Aereo Boliviano, three to LAN-Chile and five were sold to the South Manchurian Railway. One, named *Lawrence Hargrave*, was used for a short time by Airlines of Australia.

Most Ju 86s were produced as bombers, some being built by SAAB in Sweden, and it is possible that total production was about 1,000.

Last of the Junkers transports to enter airline service was the Ju 90, a large four-engined monoplane with twin fins and rudders. The prototype, *Der Grosse Dessauer*, had 1,100 hp Daimler-Benz DB 600 liquid-cooled engines and it first flew on 7 June 1937.

Production Ju 90s, the B model, had 830 hp BMW 132 air-cooled radial engines and accommodation for 38–40 passengers. In one version there were 22 or 24 seats in the main cabin and sixteen in a forward smoking cabin, but another layout had five cabins each with facing pairs of seats on each side.

The Ju 90 went into service with Lufthansa in 1938 on the Berlin–Vienna route and ten or twelve were delivered, but the war prevented their full-scale introduction. South African Airways ordered two but they were not delivered and most of the Ju 90's flying was with the Luftwaffe.

Developments of the Ju 90 were the Ju 290 and six-engined Ju 390 but these did not go into commercial service.

	Span	Length	Passengers	Loaded weight	Cruising speed	Range/ endurance
F 13	58′ 2¾″	31′ 6″	4	3,814 lb	87·0 mph	5 hr
G 24	98′ 1″	51′ 6″	9	14,330 lb	113·0 mph	807 miles
G 31	99′ 5″	56′ 8¼″	11/15	18,739 lb	105·6 mph	6 hr
W 33	58′ 2¾″	34′ 5½″	6	5,511 lb	93·2 mph	621 miles
G 38	144′ 4¼″	76′ 1¼″	34	52,911 lb	111·8 mph	2,174 miles
Ju 52/3m	95′ 11½″	62′ 0″	15/17	20,282 lb	152·2 mph	568 miles
Ju 160	46′ 11¾″	39′ 4½″	6	7,826 lb	195·7 mph	3 hr 13 min
Ju 86	73′ 10″	57′ 2½″	10	17,637 lb	223·6 mph	683 miles
Ju 90	114′ 10¾″	86′ 3½″	40	50,706 lb	198·8 mph	775/ 1,300 miles

4

The Fokker Family

The Netherlands has played a great part in the development of aviation and two names stand out as symbols of Dutch achievement. They are KLM as the world's oldest airline to retain its original name and Fokker as a great aircraft manufacturer.

Fokker developed a system of welded steel-tube fuselages and tail units married to deep ply-covered wood-framed wings and used these constructional methods for a series of outstanding transport aeroplanes which were in production until 1935 and in service until after the 1939–45 war. Most of these Fokker transport monoplanes were single-engined or three-engined, but there was one twin-engined type and two types with four engines. All but one of these aircraft had non-retractable undercarriages.

First of the Fokker transports was the V.44 (F.I) with open cockpits, but its construction was aban-doned in favour of the V.45 (F.II) which had an enclosed cabin for four passengers and a two-seat open cockpit. Like all the subsequent inter-wars Fokker transports it was a high-wing monoplane with thick-section wing covered by plywood. The fuselage was a welded steel structure with fabric covering. The original engine was a 185 hp BMW IIIa water-cooled unit but production examples had various kinds of engines including the 240 hp Siddeley Puma.

The prototype F.II was built in Germany, made its first flight in October 1919, and in March 1920 was flown to the Netherlands. The type was subsequently produced in Amsterdam and Germany and it appears that about two dozen were built. F.IIs served KLM Royal Dutch Airlines, Deutsche Luft-Reederei, Deutscher Aero Lloyd, Lufthansa,

Lufthansa's German-built Fokker F.II *Weichsel*.

Sabena and, on charter, DDL Danish Air Lines, and one was still in the Lufthansa fleet at the end of 1936. The prototype survived until the German invasion of the Netherlands in 1940.

A requirement for a somewhat larger aircraft led to the F.III which first flew in April 1921. This was very similar to the F.II but had a wider fuselage to accommodate all five passengers in the enclosed cabin. The pilot was in an open cockpit offset to one side of the centreline. The original engine was a 185 hp BMW IIIa but the 250 hp BMW IV, 240 hp Siddeley Puma and 360 hp Rolls-Royce Eagle VIII were all used, and KLM tried out the Gnome Rhône Titan and Jupiter air-cooled radial engines in two of its F.IIIs.

F.IIIs were used for several years by KLM and

in 1926 five of these were sold to Balair and made the delivery flight from Rotterdam to Switzerland in formation. Lufthansa and its predecessors used F.IIIs, Danish Air Lines had four, Hungarian and Italian airlines employed them, they operated the joint German–Russian Deruluft services linking Königsberg and Moscow, one is believed to have been used in New Guinea, and there were two in Canada and one in Alaska.

The Fokker F.IV was an enlarged F.III. It never went into airline service but it did make the first nonstop flight across the United States, flying 2,850 miles from San Diego to New York in 26 hr 51 min.

The next Fokker transport monoplane was a truly great aeroplane, the F.VII which appeared in 1924. It was much bigger than the F.II and F.III and had a cabin for eight passengers. The prototype and three of the four production aeroplanes had 360 hp Rolls-Royce Eagle IX engines and the last of the batch had a 450 hp Napier Lion. Both the Eagle and the Lion were water-cooled engines but the big step forward came in 1925 with the air-cooled radial powered F.VIIa.

The F.VIIa was an improved version of the F.VII and one of the most important early transport aeroplanes. It was fitted with a variety of engines and soon led to the three-engined F.VIIa-3m. These types were used by many European airlines, saw

service in the United States and made many important long-distance flights. The final version was the bigger F.VIIb-3m which could carry up to ten passengers. Like all the early Fokker transports the F.VIIb-3m could be powered by a wide range of engines – in this case all air-cooled radials.

The F.VII series saw service in most parts of the world and were built in the Netherlands, the United States, Belgium, Czechoslovakia, Poland, Italy and the United Kingdom. The British-built F.VIIb-3ms were known as Avro Tens and five of these were used by the pioneer Australian National Airways. One of these, *Southern Moon*, was rebuilt as C. T. P. Ulm's *Faith in Australia* and it made many outstanding flights including some across the Tasman Sea. Direct developments of the F.VIIb-3m were the United States built F-X and F-Xa which were used by a number of US airlines and by CMA in Mexico.

The most famous of the F.VIIs was the *Southern Cross*. With this blue and silver three-engined monoplane Charles Kingsford Smith, C. T. P. Ulm, Harry Lyon and James Warner made, in 1928, the first flight across the entire Pacific, from California to Brisbane via Honolulu and Fiji. The flight took 83 hr 11 min. The *Southern Cross* also made the first air crossing of the Tasman Sea, in September 1928. This great aeroplane is preserved in a special glass-

One of the large fleet of Sabena Fokker F.VIIb-3m monoplanes.

walled hall at Eagle Farm Airport, Brisbane. Another Fokker F.VII, the *Josephine Ford*, was the first aeroplane to fly over the North Pole. It achieved this on 9 May 1926, flown by Floyd Bennett and Richard E. Byrd.

F.VIIs of KLM pioneered the air route from Amsterdam to Batavia, now Jakarta.

Although of similar layout and with the standard Fokker structure, the F.VIII of 1927 was unique among pre-1939–45 war Fokker transports in having two engines. The F.VIII was heavier than the earlier types and had accommodation for fifteen passengers (later one was used for joyriding with 24 seats). Only a small number was produced, with KLM having seven and Malert, the Hungarian airline, three, of which two were built in Budapest by Manfred Weiss. One KLM F.VIII was sold to Swedish Air Lines and two to British Airways. The original engines fitted in the F.VIIIs were 480 hp Gnome Rhône Jupiter air-cooled radials, Wright Cyclones were tried in one, and eventually five of the KLM aircraft had 500 hp Pratt & Whitney Wasps.

In 1929 Fokker built the biggest of its three-engined transports, the F.IX designed for operation of KLM's services to the Netherlands East Indies (now Indonesia). Only two were built, one was lost in an accident in 1931, and the type was mostly used on European services when it had accommodation for eighteen passengers. The original engines were 480/500 hp Gnome Rhône Jupiter VIs.

Another of the outstanding Fokkers was the F.XII which first flew early in 1931. On European services the F.XII could carry sixteen passengers but its greatest service was on KLM's Far East route where it had accommodation for four passengers in sleeper-seats. Eleven F.XIIs were built by Fokker, two were delivered to KNILM in the Netherlands East Indies, eight to KLM and one to AB Aerotransport (Swedish Air Lines). Two were built

in Denmark for DDL and one of these, *Kronprinsesse Ingrid*, remained in service until 1947. Four of the KLM aircraft were sold to Crilly Airways in the United Kingdom and these were later added to the two already purchased from KLM by British Airways. The last of these was scrapped in June 1940 after passing to BOAC. The F.XII sold to Sweden, the *Värmland*, had the longest life. It remained in service with Swedish Air Lines until 1946 and was then sold to a private company for joyriding at Stockholm where at the end of that year it was destroyed in a hangar fire. *Värmland* had been built nearly three and a half years before the *Kronprinsesse Ingrid*.

The Dutch-built F.XIIs had Pratt & Whitney Wasp engines of 425/500 hp and the Danish aircraft were powered by 465 hp Bristol Jupiter VIs.

In 1932 Fokker built five F.XVIIIs for KLM's Amsterdam–Batavia service. These were similar to the F.XII but were larger and slightly faster. They had the same Eastern route accommodation as the F.XII but when replaced on the Eastern route by Douglas DC-2s in 1935 were transferred to European services with seats for thirteen passengers. Two of the F.XVIIIs made some historic long-distance flights. In 1934 the *Snip* (*Snipe*) made a 6,400 mile Christmas mail flight from Amsterdam to Curaçao in 55 hr 58 min, while the previous year the *Pelikaan*

KLM's Fokker F.XXII *Papegaai (Parrot)* at Amsterdam.

(*Pelican*) had carried Christmas mail from Amsterdam to Batavia in 4 days 4 hr 35 min with 73 hr 34 min flying time.

The F.XX which was completed in 1933 was different to all the other Fokker transports in having a retractable undercarriage, the mainwheels folding backward into the engine nacelles, that is the fairings behind the engines. It also differed from earlier Fokkers in having an elliptical-section fuselage instead of rectangular. Named *Zilvermeeuw (Silver Gull)*, having seats for twelve passengers, and originally being powered by three 640 hp Wright Cyclone engines, the F.XX was delivered to KLM in November 1933 and was normally used on the London–Amsterdam–Berlin route.

The last of the inter-wars Fokker transports were the four-engined F.XXXVI of 1934 and the F.XXII of 1935. Only one F.XXXVI was built, this was the *Arend (Eagle)*. It had accommodation for 32 passengers and four crew, was powered by four 750 hp Wright Cyclone engines and was used by KLM on the London–Amsterdam–Berlin route. Four

F.XXIIs were built, three for KLM and one for Swedish Air Lines. They were almost indistinguishable from the F.XXXVI but had accommodation for only 22 passengers and were powered by four 500 hp Pratt & Whitney Wasp engines. One KLM F.XXII was lost in an accident but the other two, together with the F.XXXVI, were all sold to the United Kingdom and served as navigational trainers with Scottish Aviation at Prestwick, and after the 1939–45 war one F.XXII was used for a short period on a Prestwick–Belfast passenger service.

The long line of Fokker transports played a major part in the development of air transport in many parts of the world but by the mid-1930s they could no longer compete with the new generation of all-metal low-wing monoplanes such as the Douglas DC-2 and DC-3.

The Fokkers designed in the United States and the recent turbine-powered F.27 Friendship and F.28 Fellowship are described later.

	Span	Length	Passengers	Loaded weight	Cruising speed	Range
F.II	52′ 10″	38′ $2\frac{3}{4}$″	4/5	4,188 lb	74·5 mph	745 miles
F.VIIa	63′ $4\frac{1}{4}$″	47′ 1″	8	8,046 lb	96·3 mph	730 miles
F.VIIb-3m	71′ $2\frac{3}{4}$″	47′ 7″	8/10	11,684 lb	110·6 mph	745 miles
F.XII	75′ $6\frac{1}{4}$″	58′ $4\frac{3}{4}$″	4/16	15,983 lb	127·3 mph	807 miles
F.XX	84′ $3\frac{3}{4}$″	54′ $9\frac{1}{2}$″	12	19,841 lb	155·3 mph	876 miles
F.XXXVI	108′ $3\frac{1}{4}$″	77′ $5\frac{1}{4}$″	32	36,376 lb	149·1 mph	838 miles
F.XXII	98′ $5\frac{1}{4}$″	70′ $7\frac{1}{4}$″	22	28,660 lb	133·5 mph	838 miles

5

From Komet to Condor

Although Junkers built more transport aeroplanes than any other German company, the products of Dornier, Focke-Wulf, Heinkel, Messerschmitt and Rohrbach all played a part in the development of German air transport.

Claudius Dornier, in charge of design at the Zeppelin-Werke Lindau, pioneered the use of duralumin and steel in a number of large military flying-boats during the First World War, and his post-war company continued to design and build outstanding flying-boats. Dornier also produced small numbers of transport landplanes, the Komet series and Merkur single-engined high-wing monoplanes. The first of these, the Komet I and II, were small four-passenger aeroplanes with very low-slung fuselages. The Komet Is had 180/185 hp BMW III engines and the Komet IIs had 250 hp BMW IV or 260 hp

Rolls-Royce Falcon engines. With the possible exception of the first Komet I, they had an open cockpit in the wing leading (or forward) edge for the pilot. Komet Is and IIs served Deutsche Luft-Reederei, Deutscher Aero Lloyd and Lufthansa, Ad Astra Aero in Switzerland, CETA in Spain, and some early Soviet airlines. Some Komet IIs were still in service in Germany in September 1928.

The Komet III, which first flew in December 1924, was a bigger aircraft with seats for six passengers. Most had 360 hp Rolls-Royce Eagle IX engines but other types could be fitted and some Komet IIIs built in Japan had Lorraine and Kawasaki-BMW engines.

In 1925 Dornier began building an improved version of the Komet III, known as the Merkur (Mercury), which had a 450/600 hp BMW VI

The Lufthansa Dornier Komet III *Edelmarder (Pine Marten)*.

engine, and many of the Komet IIIs were converted to Merkurs. Lufthansa had at least 22 Merkurs, and Merkurs or Komet IIIs were also used by Danish Air Lines, the Ukraine airline, Syndicato Condor in Brazil, Ad Astra Aero and Swissair in Switzerland, SCADTA in Colombia, Deruluft, the Chilean Air Force and some companies in Japan. In the winter of 1926–27 Walter Mittelholzer flew the Merkur *Switzerland* from Zürich to Cape Town in 100 hr flying. These aircraft could be operated on wheels or skis or as twin-float seaplanes.

Focke-Wulf, in 1924, began building the A 16 single-engined four-passenger monoplane which was a low-slung aircraft of similar design to the Dornier Komet I but of all-wooden construction. Five versions were produced, the A 16 with 75 hp Siemens & Halske Sh 11 engine, A 16a with 100 hp Mercedes D.I, A 16b with 85 hp Junkers-L 1a, A 16c with 100 hp Siemens & Halske Sh 12 and A 16d with 120 hp Mercedes D.II or D.IIa. A total of 23 of these little monoplanes was built and several worked on German internal air services, the last being withdrawn at the end of the summer of 1928.

The next Focke-Wulf design, the A 17 Möwe (Seagull), appeared in 1927. This was an eight-passenger high-wing cantilever monoplane with all-wooden wing and ply- and fabric-covered metal-framed fuselage. The engine was a 420 hp Gnome Rhône Jupiter air-cooled radial. The prototype was used by Norddeutsche Luftverkehr from 1928 on services between Bremen and German north coast resorts, twelve were built and two were still operating Lufthansa cargo services in 1935. Between 1929 and 1931 Focke-Wulf built five A 29 Möwe monoplanes. These were similar to the A 17 but had 500/750 hp BMW VI water-cooled engines. Four of the A 29s were used by Lufthansa on internal services and to Paris and Switzerland. Finally, in 1931, Focke-Wulf built four A 38 Möwe monoplanes for Lufthansa. These were similar to the earlier Möwe types but had accommodation for ten passengers and were powered by 400 hp Siemens Jupiter radial air-cooled engines. Later they had the 500 hp Siemens Sh 20u.

Another small high-wing monoplane with low-slung fuselage, on the lines of the Dornier Komet I and Focke-Wulf A 16, was the Messerschmitt M 18 which probably made its first flight in 1925. The M 18 was a three/four-passenger aircraft of metal construction with metal-skinned fuselage and metal-and fabric-covered wing, and was powered by a 110 hp Siemens & Halske Sh 12 radial. The production aircraft were the M 18a and M 18b and they were followed by the developed M 18c photographic aircraft, and the M 18ds which had eight seats, modified fuselages and undercarriages. These later versions had a variety of radial engines of 145–325 hp. Nineteen of these aircraft were used by Nordbayerische Verkehrsflug and its successor Deutsche Verkehrsflug on services radiating from Nuremberg.

A much bigger Messerschmitt was the eight/ten-passenger M 20 which had a single 500 hp BMW VIa water-cooled engine. Of all-metal construction, this type, as the M 20a, went into service with Lufthansa in 1929 on both domestic and international routes and in 1932 a number were redesignated M 20b2 when they were fitted with 640 hp BMW VIu engines. There were fourteen production aircraft and one of these was sold by Lufthansa in 1937 to the Brazilian airline Varig.

Among the pioneers of metal construction was Adolf Rohrbach and as early as May 1919 construction began of his very advanced four-engined transport, the E.4/20 with a span of 101 ft $8\frac{1}{2}$ in and a cruising speed of 124 mph. It was completed in September 1920 but the Allied Control Commission ordered it to be grounded and it was broken

The Lufthansa Rohrbach Roland II *Siegburg*.

up in 1922 without going into service.

Much of Rohrbach's future work was on all-metal flying-boats, but in 1926 the Ro VIII Roland three-engined landplane appeared. This was a high-wing monoplane with accommodation for ten passengers. The first version was powered by three 230 hp BMW IV water-cooled engines and had an open cockpit, then came the Ro VIIIa with covered cockpit and 320 hp BMW Va engines and, finally, the Ro VIIIb Roland II with completely redesigned crew cabin. Eighteen of these aircraft were used by Lufthansa

and some remained in service until 1936. Four or five of the Lufthansa aircraft subsequently went to Spain and at least three were used by the Russo–German airline Deruluft.

One of the most beautiful European transport aeroplanes was the Heinkel He 70 'Blitz' (Lightning) which first flew in December 1932. The low canti-lever wing was elliptical in plan and of all-wooden construction, and the finely streamlined fuselage was of metal. The cabin had four seats and there was a crew of two. The mainwheels retracted out-

The special Focke-Wulf Condor which flew nonstop from Berlin to New York in 1938.

wards to lie flat in the wing. With a speed of up to 223 mph, the He 70 was claimed to be the fastest passenger aircraft in Europe.

The Heinkel He 70s were powered by 630/750 hp BMW VI liquid-cooled engines and from June 1934 operated Lufthansa's express services linking Berlin, Hamburg, Cologne and Frankfurt-am-Main. Later they worked on other routes and some remained in service until 1938.

A twin-engined development of the He 70 was the He 111 which is best remembered as a Luftwaffe bomber. In outline the He 111 was generally similar to the He 70 but was powered by two 750 hp BMW VIu engines and had accommodation for ten passengers, four of them in a smoking cabin. He 111s entered service with Lufthansa on domestic express services in 1936 and began working on international routes in 1937. At least one was used on some sectors of the German South Atlantic mail service.

An outstanding German transport monoplane was the Focke-Wulf Fw 200 Condor which first flew in July 1937 and entered service with Danish Air Lines and Lufthansa in the summer of 1938. The Condor was a four-engined all-metal low-wing cantilever monoplane with accommodation for 25–26 passengers in two cabins. The engines were 720/830 hp BMW 132 air-cooled radials and the undercarriage, including the tailwheel, was fully retractable.

The Condor was the first four-engined transport landplane to fly the North Atlantic. In August 1938 one of them flew nonstop from Berlin to New York in 24 hr 56 min and returned in 19 hr 55 min. At the end of 1938 the same aircraft flew from Berlin to Tokyo in 46 hr 18 min with intermediate stops only at Basra, Karachi and Hanoi.

In addition to the Lufthansa and Danish Condors, the type was ordered by Syndicato Condor and by Aero O/Y in Finland. The Finnish order was not met, but two Condors did go to Brazil, then passed to Cruzeiro do Sul, and remained in airline service until April 1947. Somewhere between 250 and 300 Condors are believed to have been built but most of them were used as bomber-reconnaissance aircraft by the Luftwaffe. Had it not been for the war it is likely that the Condor would have been widely used by Lufthansa and probably exported in some numbers. Most Condors were used for long-range patrol work over the Atlantic.

	Span	Length	Passengers	Loaded weight	Cruising speed	Range
Dornier Komet I	55′ 9¼″	31′ 2″	4	4,519 lb	80·7 mph	372 miles
Dornier Merkur	64′ 3½″	41′ 0″	6	7,936 lb	111·8 mph	—
Rohrbach Roland I	86′ 3½″	52′ 10″	10	15,763 lb	108·7 mph	932 miles
Focke-Wulf A 17 Möwe	65′ 7¼″	42′ 7¾″	8	7,958 lb	93·2 mph	435 miles
Messerschmitt M 20b	83′ 8″	52′ 2″	10	10,141 lb	95·6 mph	620 miles
Focke-Wulf A 38 Möwe	65′ 7¼″	50′ 6¼″	10	9,700 lb	105·6 mph	466 miles
Heinkel He 70	48′ 6½″	39′ 4½″	4	7,628 lb	189·5 mph	621 miles
Heinkel He 111	74′ 1¾″	57′ 5″	10	17,350 lb	189·5 mph	621 miles
Focke-Wulf Fw 200 Condor	108′ 3¼″	78′ 3″	25/26	37,479 lb	226·7 mph	932 miles

6

French Creations

Well over a hundred types of French-designed and built aircraft are known to have been operated on France's scheduled passenger, mail and cargo air services since 1919. These range from the converted wartime aircraft described in Chapter 1 to the Caravelle twin-jets of the present day. With such a wide range of aircraft it is only possible here to describe briefly a few of the more important types.

For the most part the French transports can be broken down into a number of categories: single-engined biplanes used on European services; multi-engined biplanes for European use; some single- and multi-engined monoplanes used in Europe; the Latécoère family of aircraft used to develop the great pioneering route through West Africa to South America; the standard fleets of multi-engined monoplanes used in the 1930s; the big South Atlantic Farmans; and the post World War II types.

In 1919 Blériot built the sleek two-passenger wood and fabric Spad 27 single-engined biplane powered by a 300 hp Hispano Suiza engine. Three of these little aeroplanes were used on Paris–London services and they had a top speed of more than 140 mph. From the Spad 27 was developed a whole series of compact single-engined passenger biplanes. They all had streamlined circular-section fuselages with a passenger cabin amidship and open cockpits for the pilot and a mechanic or extra passenger. The wings were of unequal span and the structures were of wood with fabric-covered wings and tails. Most of these aircraft had four-seat cabins but the later versions had seats for six passengers.

The first of these Blériots were the Spad 33s which began to appear in 1920; forty were produced

A Jupiter-engined Blériot Spad 56 used on Central European services by CIDNA.

and they had 230/260 hp Salmson water-cooled radial engines. In 1921 came the Spad 46 with 370 hp Lorraine-Dietrich 12Da engine and at least fifty were built. Then came the five Hispano Suiza engined Spad 50s. The Spad 56 of 1923 was the first of the series to have an air-cooled engine – the Gnome Rhône Jupiter – and the type remained in production until 1929. The Spad 66s were modified Spad 33s and 46s. Finally there was one Spad 116 with 450 hp Renault engine and one Spad 126 with a 450 hp Hispano Suiza. At least 107 of these

Blériot Spads were built and they were used by numerous French airlines and in Belgium by SNETA and Sabena. Their most important task was with Cie Franco-Roumaine de Navigation Aérienne and CIDNA on the development of routes which eventually extended from Paris to Constantinople (now Istanbul) via Strasbourg, Zürich, Innsbruck, Vienna, Budapest, Belgrade and Bucharest, with a branch from Vienna to Prague and Warsaw.

Although the Blériot Spads did good work on these eastern European routes, they were first served by two types of single-engined Potez biplanes, the two-passenger Potez S.E.A. VII and the Potez IX. It is also of interest that in 1929 CIDNA replaced the Spads with another Potez, the type 29. This was a five/six-seat cabin biplane produced in two main versions, one with 450 hp Lorraine-Dietrich water-cooled and the other with the 420/480 hp Gnome Rhône Jupiter air-cooled engine. CIDNA, Aeroput of Yugoslavia, LARES of Rumania, Aéropostale and Aeroposta Argentina all used Potez 29s and at least 23 were built.

Developed from the Potez 29 biplane was the Potez 32 two/five-passenger strut-braced high-wing monoplane. About thirty of these wooden aircraft were built, some with 230 hp Salmson 9Ab and some with 380 hp Gnome Rhône Jupiter air-cooled engines. CIDNA had eleven Potez 32s, Air Orient had three based at Saïgon and the type was also used by Aéropostale and Air Asie.

Another French single-engined transport biplane which deserves mention is the Breguet 280T. At least nineteen were built, in three versions, and under the class name *Rapid Azur* they served Air Union and its successor Air France, mostly on the Paris–Lyons–Marseilles, Lyons–Geneva and Paris–London routes, from 1929. These unequal span biplanes had metal structures with mixed metal and fabric covering, carried a crew of two and had seats for eight passengers. The Breguet 280T had a 500 hp Renault engine, the 281T a 450 hp Lorraine-Dietrich and the 284T a 580 hp Hispano Suiza – all were water-cooled. The 282T and 283T were planned to have air-cooled Gnome Rhône Jupiters but neither version is known to have been built.

One of the sagas of air transport is that of the development of French air services to South America. The task was begun by Lignes Aériennes Latécoère and its successors Cie Générale Aéropostale and Air France and a number of subsidiary companies in Brazil and the Argentine. Two single-engined biplanes, the Latécoère 3 Postal and Latécoère 8, played a small part in this work, but the biggest contribution was made by a series of Latécoère single-engined high-wing monoplanes and, later, by flying-boats.

The first of the Latécoère monoplanes to see large-scale service was the Laté 17 which appeared in 1924. This was a strut-braced monoplane of mixed construction with metal-covered cabin section. Although mainly used for mail these aeroplanes could carry four passengers. The Laté 17R had a 300/450 hp Renault water-cooled engine and the Laté 17J a 380 hp air-cooled Gnome Rhône Jupiter. A slightly modified version, the Laté 25, had a larger wing and a 450/500 hp Renault engine with frontal radiator or a Gnome Rhône Jupiter. The final version was the Laté 26 which had a redesigned fuselage, was intended for mail carriage but could carry two passengers, and was powered by a Renault engine. It appears that at least 136 of these Latécoère monoplanes were built, they were painted silver and red, and operated between France and West Africa and in South America but did not operate over the ocean.

In 1929 a much larger Latécoère monoplane, the Laté 28, appeared, some fifty or so were built, and these were introduced on the services to West Africa and in South America. They were braced high-wing monoplanes, had seats for up to eight passengers and were powered by a single 500/650 hp Hispano Suiza water-cooled engine. At least seven Laté 28s were operated as twin-float seaplanes and one of these, *Comte de la Vaulx*, flew the ocean sector from

Sénégal to Brazil with the first experimental all-air mail from Toulouse to Rio de Janeiro. The captain on that flight, in May 1930, was the famous Jean Mermoz and the ocean crossing took 21 hr.

In the 1920s France built several types of twin- and three-engined transport biplanes which were, in general, similar in layout to the British Handley Pages and Armstrong Whitworth Argosy. One series was designed and built by Caudron. These were the three-engined C.61, C.61bis (or second), C.81 and C.183, all wooden aircraft with fabric covering and seats for six to eight passengers. All were used on the central European routes by either Cie Franco-Roumaine or CIDNA. The C.61s entered service in 1923 on night services between Belgrade and Bucharest and were powered by 180 hp Hispano Suiza engines. In 1924 some had their outboard engines replaced by 260 hp Salmsons when they were designated C.61bis. The C.81s were rather larger than the C.61s, had a 400 hp Lorraine-Dietrich engine in the nose and 260 hp Salmsons in the outboard positions and entered service in 1924. Only one C.183 is known, it had one Lorraine and two Salmson engines, was delivered in 1925 and based at Vienna. The total number of these three-engined Caudrons is believed to have been eighteen.

Best remembered of the French multi-engined biplanes, after the Farman Goliath, is the Lioré et Olivier 21. This was an equal-span square-tipped biplane with two six-seat cabins and an open cockpit. It was powered by two 450/500 hp Renault water-cooled engines and had a partly enclosed undercarriage. Painted red and gold, a fleet of thirteen LeO 21s served Air Union, mainly on the Paris–London and Paris–Lyons–Marseilles routes, under the fleet title le 'Rayon d'Or' (The Golden Ray). The type entered service in 1929 and finished its civil career as a cargo aircraft with Air France in 1934, after which nine passed to the French Air Force as troop carriers.

A French aeroplane which must be mentioned, if only for its extreme ugliness, is the Farman Jabiru (Stork). The F.121 Jabiru was a fantastic looking aeroplane which got even uglier as it was developed. It was a strut-braced high-wing monoplane with a very thick wide-chord* wing and this was married to a very deep slab-sided fuselage. The prototype, which appeared in 1923, had four water-cooled engines mounted in tandem pairs low-down above the mainwheels and carried on short stub-wings.

In 1926 the Farman Line and Danish Air Lines put the F-3X version of the Jabiru into service. This was powered by four 180 hp Hispano Suiza engines and had accommodation for nine passengers

* The chord is the measurement from the leading to the trailing edge of the wing.

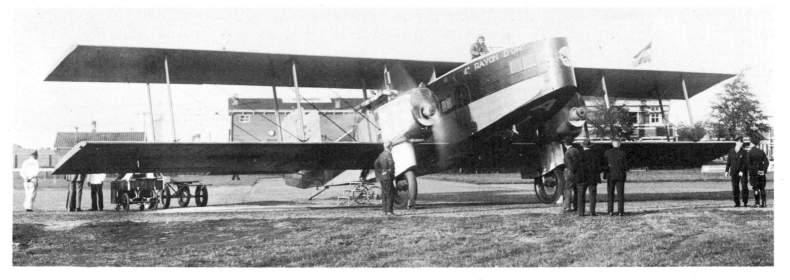

One of Air Union's red and gold Lioré et Olivier 21 *Golden Ray* biplanes.
This is the LeO 213 version.

with two of the seats in a cabin in the extreme nose. These were almost certainly the first four-engined airliners to go into regular service anywhere. Danish Air Lines actually had two Jabirus specially built in Copenhagen.

Even uglier than the four-engined Jabirus was the F-4X three-engined version, four of which were used by CIDNA from early 1925. This version dispensed with the front cabin and instead had a 300 hp uncowled Salmson AZ.9 engine mounted in the top of the nose, with two others close beside the nose mounted forward of the stub-wing.

A smaller single-engined version of the Jabiru, the F.170, was also produced. This could carry eight passengers and was normally powered by a 500 hp Farman 12We water-cooled engine. This type appeared in 1925 and Farman Line employed at least thirteen as well as six of the slightly larger F.170bis, mostly on the Paris–Cologne–Berlin route.

Farman also built the F.300 series of braced high-wing monoplanes, the first of which flew in 1930. These were wood and fabric aircraft with accommodation for eight passengers. The first batch, each with three 230 hp Salmson engines, were the F.301s, and Farman Line used six of them on its Paris–Berlin and Paris–Copenhagen–Malmö services. There were also six F.303s each with three 240 hp Gnome Rhône Titan engines and smaller numbers of the F.302 (one 650 hp Hispano Suiza), F.304 (three Lorraine 9Na), F.305 (two Gnome Rhône Titans and one Jupiter), F.306 (three Lorraine 7Me) and the F.310 (three Salmson 9Ab). In service with Farman the F.300 series bore the fleet name *l'Étoile d'Argent* (*The Silver Star*).

A number of large four-engined monoplanes were built by Farman for transatlantic mail operation. These were the F.220, F.2200, F.2220, F.2231 and F.2234, but they were not used for passenger carriage. The four-engined F.224 was designed as a forty-passenger aeroplane for Air France, but the airline rejected it and all six are thought to have been taken over by the French Air Force.

In 1933 Air Union introduced on the Paris–London route an advanced three-engined all-metal low-wing monoplane under the fleet name *la Voile d'Or* (*The Golden Clipper*). This was the ten-passenger Wibault 282.T12 powered by three Gnome Rhône Titan Major air-cooled radial engines. When Air France was founded in October 1933 it took over the Wibaults and eventually had a fleet of eighteen

including ten of the model 283.T12 which were heavier and had increased fuel capacity. Painted silver and dark blue, the Wibaults operated on Air France's main European routes and in South America. At least one was fitted with an experimental retractable undercarriage.

Another early Air France transport was the high-wing fourteen/sixteen-passenger Potez 62 of mixed construction and having a retractable undercarriage. The first version was the Potez 62-0 with two 870 hp Gnome Rhône Mistral Major radial engines and this was followed by the 62-1 with 720 hp Hispano Suiza liquid-cooled engines. Air France had a fleet of 22 Potez 62s and they first went into service in June 1935 on the Paris–Marseilles–Rome route. Later they worked on numerous European routes, across the Andes between Buenos Aires and Santiago, and in the Far East.

In 1933 Air France took delivery of the three-engined all-metal cantilever monoplane *Émeraude* (*Emerald*). This was the Dewoitine D.332 and it made a number of very fast flights in Europe, to West Africa and Saïgon, but on its return flight from the Far East it was destroyed in an accident in bad weather. From the D.332 was developed the similar eight/ten-passenger D.333. Air France had three D.333s, one being used between Toulouse and Dakar and two in South America. Next came

The Air France Wibault 283.T12 *Le Glorieux (The Glorious)* at Le Bourget, Paris.

the D.338 with retractable undercarriage and seats for up to 22 passengers. Air France had a fleet of thirty of these Dewoitines and the first one entered service in the summer of 1936. The D.338s worked in Europe, between Damascus and Hanoi, over the African section of the South America route, and from August 1938 to Hongkong. Nine D.338s survived the war and the type remained in service with Air France until the end of 1946. The engines were 650 hp Hispano Suiza air-cooled radials.

The winter of 1937–38 saw the introduction by Air France of a replacement for its Wibaults. This was the twin-engined all-metal Bloch 220 low-wing monoplane. These had retractable undercarriages, seats for sixteen passengers, and were powered by two 915/985 hp Gnome Rhône 14N radial engines. Bloch 220s were introduced on the Paris–London route in March 1938 and cut the scheduled time for the journey from $1\frac{1}{2}$ to $1\frac{1}{4}$ hr. Sixteen were used by Air France and several were still in service in 1949 by which time they had become Bloch 221s with American Wright Cyclone engines.

An aircraft which served France well for several years from May 1946 was the SNCASE SE.161 Languedoc four-engined low-wing monoplane, although it went through some troublesome times during its development. The Languedoc originated in a 1936 requirement for a Colonial transport for Air Afrique and began life as the Bloch 161 which first flew in September 1939. Because of the war the first production aeroplane did not fly until September 1945. It had by then become the Sud-Est 161. Air France ordered forty to replace its Bloch 220s and Dewoitines and in May 1946 the Languedocs went into service between Paris and Algiers.

Initially the Languedoc was powered by four

Gnome Rhône 14N radial engines but most aircraft were modified to have 1,220 hp Pratt & Whitney R-1830s. Two cabins provided accommodation for 33 passengers but in 1951 Air France increased capacity on its remaining Languedocs to 44 and used them on second-class services to North Africa. A total of a hundred Languedocs was built of which five went to Polskie Linie Lotnicze 'LOT'. Others were used by Air Liban, Air Atlas, Aviaco, Misrair and Tunis Air.

Less successful than the Languedoc was the SE.2010 Armagnac. This was the outcome of a study, begun in 1942, for an aeroplane capable of carrying 87 passengers between Marseilles and Algiers or 32 in berths over the ocean section of the South America route. Later the design was changed to allow carriage of 64 passengers over the North Atlantic, or 107 on short routes. The prototype flew in April 1949 and production of fifteen aircraft was begun for Air France, but the airline decided against the Armagnac and its main operations were confined to carrying military supplies from France to Indo-China.

The Armagnac was an all-metal mid-wing cantilever monoplane powered by four 3,500 hp Pratt & Whitney Wasp Majors. It could carry 84 first-class passengers or with high-density seating 160 passengers.

An unusual but successful French aeroplane was the Breguet 763 Deux-Ponts. This was a large mid-wing monoplane powered by four 2,100/2,400 hp Pratt & Whitney R-2800 engines and having passenger accommodation on two decks – 59 in tourist class seats on the top deck and 48 second class on the lower deck. The two decks were connected by a stairway. Large doors under the rear fuselage made possible the loading of bulky cargo or vehicles.

The Deux-Ponts first flew in February 1949 and the developed production version entered service with Air France in March 1953. The airline had twelve of these aircraft which were operated, mainly between France and North Africa, under the name Provence. After more than ten years of reliable operation six went to the French Air Force and the others were converted to Universal freighters each with a payload of about fifteen tons.

	Span	Length	Passengers	Loaded weight	Cruising speed	Range
Blériot Spad 33	38′ 3″	29′ 9½″	4/5	4,545 lb	99·4 mph	671 miles
Latécoère 17R	45′ 11¼″	31′ 5¼″	4	4,784 lb	87·0 mph	310 miles
Farman F-3X Jabiru	62′ 4″	44′ 10½″	9	11,023 lb	108·7 mph	403 miles
Breguet 280T	56′ 7″	39′ 9″	8	7,319 lb	123·0 mph	683 miles
Latécoère 28	63′ 1¼″	44′ 3½″	8	8,501 lb	120·0 mph	621 miles
Lioré et Olivier 21	76′ 10½″	52′ 4″	12	12,566 lb	108·7 mph	347 miles
Potez 29	47′ 7″	34′ 9½″	5	5,511 lb	127·3 mph	310 miles
Wibault 282.T12	74′ 2″	55′ 9¼″	10	13,668 lb	124·2 mph	652 miles
Potez 62-0	73′ 7¾″	56′ 10″	14/16	16,534 lb	173·9 mph	621 miles
Dewoitine D.338	96′ 3½″	72′ 7¼″	12/22	24,581 lb	161·5 mph	1,211 miles
Bloch 220	74′ 10½″	63′ 1¾″	16	20,943 lb	173·9 mph	869 miles
SE.161 Languedoc	96′ 4¾″	79′ 6¾″	33/44	51,360 lb	211·2 mph	621 miles
SE.2010 Armagnac	160′ 7″	130′ 0″	84/160	170,858 lb	282·1 mph	1,522 miles
Breguet 763	141′ 0½″	94′ 11½″	107	113,758 lb	208·7 mph	1,423 miles

7

Italian Landplanes

Italy, with its long Mediterranean and Adriatic coastlines and its northern lakes, was almost ideal for the operation of marine aircraft so long as its air services were confined to the general Mediterranean area, and as a consequence most of the early Italian air services were operated by flying-boats and they, together with seaplanes, remained in commercial operation up to the start of the 1939–45 war.

However, as Italian air routes were extended into continental Europe and as air services were developed in Italy's African territories it became necessary to add landplane transports to the civil air fleets. Initially Fokker and Junkers equipment was used, but the increasing landplane requirement led to home design and manufacture and Caproni, Fiat and Savoia Marchetti all produced families of transport landplanes.

The long-established Caproni concern began in 1928 construction of the Ca 97 strut-braced high-wing monoplane for civil and military use. The prototype is believed to have been powered by three 100/130 hp Lorraine-Dietrich radial engines and to have been used by Avio Linee Italiane. The Ca 97 had a cabin for six passengers and was fitted with a range of different engines. A version with three 145 hp Walter Mars engines was used by SAM and Ala Littoria and by ČSA in Czechoslovakia. A Ca 97 with a single Piaggio Jupiter engine was used on Milan–Verona–Padua–Venice services and a few Jupiter-powered examples were built in Hungary.

An enlarged version of the Ca 97 was the eight-passenger Ca 101 which was first produced in 1930.

Two Ca 101s each with three Alfa Romeo Lynx engines and three each powered by one Alfa Romeo Jupiter and two Lynx engines were employed on the Tripoli–Benghazi and Benghazi–Tobruk services of Societa Nord-Africa Aviazione – four of these passed to Ala Littoria, SAM used a Ca 101 with three Walter Castor engines, and Malert in Hungary had at least two twin-engined Ca 101s.

A development of the Ca 101 was the more advanced Ca 133 which appeared in 1935. This was of similar layout to its predecessors but had a spatted* undercarriage and camber-changing flaps. It is believed that not less than 275 of these aircraft were built but not many were used for civil duties. Ala Littoria had at least twelve and used them on the Rome–Addis Ababa route and on a network of services in East Africa. The Ca 133 was powered by three 460 hp Piaggio Stella air-cooled radial engines and, like the Ca 97 and Ca 101, was of steel-tube construction with fabric covering, although the forward fuselage of the Ca 133 differed from the earlier types in having a metal skin.

Fiat flew its three-engined four/seven-passenger G.2 in July 1932 and its twin-engined twelve-passenger APR.2 in 1935. The former was used by Avio Linee Italiane on domestic services and the latter by the same airline on its Venice–Milan–Paris route, but only one of each type was built.

Fiat's first transport aeroplane to go into production was its eighteen-passenger G.18 which first flew in March 1935. This was a twin-engined low-wing monoplane with retractable undercarriage. It was an all-metal aircraft and was produced in two versions, the G.18 with 700 hp Fiat A.59R and the G.18 V with 1,000 hp Fiat A.80 RC.41 air-cooled radial engines. Three G.18s were built and they entered service with Avio Linee Italiane in 1936, to be joined in 1937 by the six G.18 Vs. They were used on domestic and international services based on Milan and, in June 1938, began operating the first Italian air services to the United Kingdom – from Venice to Croydon via Milan, Turin and Paris.

All subsequent production Fiat transports were three-engined low-wing monoplanes of a related series. The first was the G.12 which first flew in October 1940. It was designed for Avio Linee Italiane's routes which involved Alpine crossings and built in several versions, including the G.12 LGA intended for operation of LATI's services to South America. The G.12 RT variant was designed for *nonstop* operation between Rome and Tokyo.

Three G.12s were delivered to Avio Linee Italiane in 1943. After the war the Italian airline 'Airone' had four G.12 Ls which passed to Ali Flotte Riunite, and Alitalia operated four G.12 Ls and five G.12 LBs. The G.12 L had 770 hp Fiat A.74 RC.42

* Spats were streamlined fairings used to enclose the wheels, thereby increasing an aircraft's speed.   *Italian Landplanes*

An Avio Linee Italiane Fiat G.212 CP Aeropullman Monterosa.

engines and the G.12 LB had 730 hp Bristol Pegasus 48 engines. Passenger accommodation was for 16 to 22. The Alitalia G.12 Ls had cargo panniers beneath their fuselages.

The Fiat G.212, which first flew in January 1947, was similar to the G.12 series but was larger and heavier. Avio Linee Italiane, later part of Ali Flotte Riunite, and the Egyptian airline SAIDE operated the 34-passenger G.212 CP Aeropullman Monterosa version which had three 1,065 hp Pratt & Whitney Twin Wasp engines and underfloor and wing leading-

edge baggage holds. Seating was in pairs on the starboard side with single seats on the port side. Only nine are known to have been used in airline service.

Savoia Marchetti had built a long line of flying-boats before the appearance of its first landplane transport which first flew in 1930. This was the three-engined high-wing cantilever monoplane S.71 which had accommodation for up to ten passengers. These aircraft had non-retractable undercarriages and single fins and rudders. They could be powered by

Two Avio Linee Italiane Savoia Marchetti S.73s at Milan.

three 240 hp Walter Castor or three 370 hp Piaggio Stella air-cooled radial engines, and resembled Fokkers.

SAM had four Castor-powered and two Stella-engined S.71s and the first of these entered service on the Rome–Brindisi route. Later, S.71s operated the entire route from Rome to Salonica. At least five passed to Ala Littoria and four were still in service until 1937. The S.71's wing was of wood with ply covering and the fuselage and tail unit were fabric-covered metal structures.

The S.74, which first flew in November 1934, was also a high-wing cantilever monoplane and was of similar construction to the S.71, but it had four 700 hp Piaggio Stella or 845 hp Alfa Romeo Pegasus engines. Three of these 24-passenger aircraft were built for Ala Littoria and used on Rome–Paris services. Passenger oxygen was supplied for the Alps crossings.

Built in much larger numbers than the S.71 and S.74 was the three-engined low-wing S.73 which entered service with Sabena in the summer of 1935.

The S.73 had a very thick section all-wood watertight wing and a fabric-covered steel-tube fuselage. The cabin occupied a much bigger percentage of the fuselage than in previous types and comprised a main fourteen-seat saloon and a smaller four-seat forward section. The undercarriage was not retractable but the mainwheels were enclosed in large streamlined spats.

The engines used in the S.73s were 600 hp Gnome Rhône Mistral Majors, 670/700 hp Piaggio Stellas, 550/760 hp Wright Cyclones, 800 hp Alfa Romeo 126 RC.10s and 550/615 hp Walter Pegasus.

S.73s were used by Sabena, Ala Littoria, Avio Linee Italiane, and ČSA. At least forty were built in Italy and SABCA in Belgium built seven to give Sabena a total of twelve.

Of similar appearance to the S.73 but larger and with a retractable undercarriage was the S.M.75 which first flew in November 1937. This type was powered by three 750 hp Alfa Romeo 126 RC.34 engines and had accommodation for up to thirty passengers. About fifty of these aircraft were built, most of them going to Ala Littoria, but five were supplied to the Hungarian airline Malert and these had Gnome Rhône engines. At least one Ala Littoria S.M.75 was fitted with twin floats as the S.M.87.

Last of the Savoia Marchetti three-engined low-wing monoplanes to go into airline service was the S.M.83 which was a passenger-carrying version of the S.79 bomber. About twenty-two civil S.M.83s were built. Three were used by Sabena, from November 1938, on services between Brussels and the Belgian Congo, three were used by LARES in Rumania and at least ten were used by LATI to operate the first Italian air services to South America – the first commercial ocean crossing being made on 23 December 1939. On short-stage work the S.M.83s had accommodation for up to ten passengers. The engines used were 750 hp Alfa Romeo 126 RC.34s and, in the Sabena aircraft, 810/1,000 hp Wright Cyclones. S.M.83s operated the South Atlantic services weekly until 1942.

The biggest of all the Savoia Marchetti civil transports was the S.M.95. Still of similar construction to the early types, with all-wooden wing, the S.M.95 was a four-engined low-wing monoplane with retractable undercarriage. The prototype first flew in May 1943 and this and the first two production aeroplanes were used as military transports. After the war a modified 20/26-passenger version was produced and six were delivered to Alitalia – one being used to open the Rome–Northolt service on 3 April 1948. Another three were used by LATI on services linking Rome and Venezuela, and yet another three, possibly with seats for 38 passengers, were used by SAIDE on services from Cairo through North Africa, and to Italy, Greece and France.

Alfa Romeo 128 RC.18 engines each of 850 hp, 740 hp Bristol Pegasus 48s and 1,065 hp Pratt & Whitney Twin Wasps were all used in the S.M.95s. Oxygen was available for passengers on high altitude flights.

	Span		Length		Passengers	Loaded weight	Cruising speed	Range
Caproni Ca 133	69′	8″	50′	$4\frac{3}{4}''$	16	14,385 lb	142·9 mph	838 miles
Fiat G.18 V	82′	$0\frac{1}{4}''$	61′	$8\frac{1}{2}''$	18	23,809 lb	211·2 mph	1,025 miles
Fiat G.12 L	94′	$2\frac{3}{4}''$	73′	$6\frac{1}{2}''$	16/22	34,171 lb	193·8 mph	1,522 miles
Fiat G.212 CP	96′	3″	75′	$7\frac{1}{2}''$	34	38,360 lb	186·4 mph	1,550 miles
Savoia Marchetti S.73	78′	9″	57′	3″	18	22,993 lb	173·9 mph	633 miles
Savoia Marchetti S.74	97′	$4\frac{1}{2}''$	70′	1″	24	30,865 lb	186·4 mph	621 miles
Savoia Marchetti S.M.75	97′	$5\frac{1}{2}''$	73′	2″	24/30	31,967 lb	201·9 mph	1,416 miles
Savoia Marchetti S.M.83	69′	$6\frac{3}{4}''$	53′	$1\frac{3}{4}''$	6/10	22,707 lb	248·5 mph	995 miles
Savoia Marchetti S.M.95	112′	$5\frac{3}{4}''$	81′	3″	20/26	47,641 lb	173·9 mph	1,242 miles

8

Post Office 'Jenny' to DC-3

The United States had a regular scheduled air service before any other country. It was a flying-boat service between St Petersburg and Tampa in Florida and it started in January 1914 but survived for only four months. Then on 15 May 1918, the US Army began operating a mail service between New York and Washington via Philadelphia using Curtiss JN-4 'Jenny' training biplanes. The US Post Office took over the operation in August 1918 and then began the task of providing a complete transcontinental air mail service, opening the first sector, between Chicago and Cleveland, on 15 May 1919. The route was completed with the opening of the Omaha–Sacramento stage on 8 September 1920. The aircraft used by the Post Office were mostly modified American-built D.H.4s.

Early in 1926 mail contracts began to be awarded to commercial airlines and within a year a dozen companies were operating mail services in various parts of the country with a wide assortment of single-engined aeroplanes including the Douglas M-2 biplane and the Fokker Universal and Stout 2-AT monoplanes. A start had also been made on the establishment of passenger services.

Then in January 1927 contracts began to be awarded by the Post Office for commercial operation of the transcontinental route and this led to the first of the long line of Boeing transports which developed from small single-engined biplanes up to today's family of jet transports including the latest Boeing 747. Twenty-five Boeing Model 40A single-engined biplanes were built for operation over the San Francisco–Chicago section of the route. These were powered by the 420 hp Pratt & Whitney

◄ One of Maddux Airlines' Ford Tri-motors – the famous Tin Goose.

Wasp engine and could carry pilot, 1,200 lb of mail and two passengers. This type was progressively improved (some were able to carry four passengers), 76 are believed to have been built, including five in Canada, and they were used by Boeing Air Transport, Pacific Air Transport and Western Canada Airways. Two have been preserved, one in the Ford Museum at Dearborn and the other in Chicago.

The successful operation of the Boeing 40s showed the need for aircraft with much increased passenger accommodation, and this led, in 1928, to the production of the twelve-passenger Boeing Model 80 with three 410 hp Pratt & Whitney Wasp engines. These Boeings were quite big biplanes of metal construction with fabric covering and four were built. Next came ten Model 80As with 525 hp Hornet engines and seats for eighteen passengers, and the earlier aircraft were brought up to this standard.

A number of United States airlines employed Fokker monoplanes, some built in the Netherlands but most of American manufacture. F.VII single- and three-engined types, as described in Chapter 4, were used and when Pan American Airways began its first regular services, in October 1927, between Key West in Florida and Havana, the company used F.VIIa-3m monoplanes.

Developed directly from the F.VII series was the slightly bigger F-X three-engined twelve-passenger type which was only built in the United States. It entered service in May 1928 on Western Air Express's Los Angeles–San Francisco route and it is believed that at least 64 F-X and F-Xa transports were built. They were used by a number of airlines in the USA, Canada and Mexico.

In production at the same time as the F.VII/F-X series were the smaller Universal and Super Universal, the first of which appeared in 1925.

The Universal was a four/six-passenger strut-braced monoplane powered by a Wright Whirlwind engine, and the Super Universal was a slightly larger seven-passenger cantilever monoplane normally powered by a 410 hp Pratt & Whitney Wasp engine. Forty-five Universals and 81 US-built Super Universals were produced and many saw airline service, particularly in the United States, Canada, Central America and Japan. Super Universals were also built in Canada and Japan.

In 1929 the Fokker F-XIV went into production mainly for mail carriage but with seats for seven to nine passengers. The F-XIV was similar to previous Fokker thick-wing monoplanes but had a parasol wing and, unusually, the pilot occupied an open cockpit aft of the wing. The type could be powered by either a Pratt & Whitney Hornet or a Wright Cyclone radial engine, about twenty were built and most were used by Western Air Express and Western Canada Airways.

The last, and the biggest, of all the American Fokker transports was the F-32 which entered service with Universal Air Lines and Western Air Express in 1930. The F-32 had a rectangular-section fuselage on which was mounted a broad and very thick wing. The tailplane carried twin fins and rudders and the undercarriage was non-retractable. The four 425 hp Pratt & Whitney Hornet air-cooled engines were carried on struts in tandem pairs beneath the wing. There were seats for 32 passengers and these were arranged in pairs on each side of a central aisle. At the time they were built the F-32s were the biggest American transport aeroplanes and seven were produced.

Developed at the same time as the F-32, was the Curtiss Condor twin-engined eighteen-passenger equal-span biplane. This was a fabric-covered metal aircraft powered by two 600 hp Curtiss Conqueror liquid-cooled engines and having biplane tail, twin fins and rudders and non-retractable undercarriage. Six were built, and they were used by Transcontinental Air Transport (TAT) and Eastern Air Transport (later Eastern Air Lines). Known as the CO or Model 18, the civil Condor was a development of the Condor bomber.

A second type of Curtiss Condor, which first flew in January 1933, was also a twin-engined biplane but was a completely new design. This was the T-32 with unequal-span wings, Wright Cyclone radial engines, single fin and rudder and retractable undercarriage. It was produced in several versions, could carry fifteen passengers by day or twelve as a sleeper, and 45 were built. Most of the T-32 series Condors were initially used by Eastern Air Transport and American Airways (later American Airlines), but within a very short time they had to compete with modern all-metal monoplanes and were sold to non-American operators. A Condor was operated by Swissair and four were used on cargo services by the British company International Air Freight. Two Condors were used by Admiral Byrd's 1939 Antarctic Expedition and one was abandoned there in 1941 – it is almost certainly still there, encased in ice and snow.

One of the best known of the early United States transport aeroplanes was the Ford Tri-motor, known as the Tin Goose. This was a cantilever high-wing monoplane with thick wing and all-metal structure completely covered by a corrugated metal skin. The Tri-motor traces its origin to the single-engined Stout 2-AT which first flew in 1924 and entered service as a freighter on 13 April 1925, over the Dearborn–Chicago route. At least eleven were used, by Ford, by Stout Air Services, and Florida Airways.

One of the 2-ATs was modified to become the 3-AT with three Wright Whirlwind engines and in this configuration was nearly as ugly as the French three-engined Farman Jabiru.

The next development was the Ford 4-AT Tri-motor which first flew on 11 June 1926, and entered service with Ford Freight Line on 14 December 1926. The type underwent continuous development and there were numerous variants but most used were the 4-AT and 5-AT series. Most of the 4-ATs were powered by 200/300 hp Wright Whirlwinds and the 5-ATs by 400/450 hp Pratt & Whitney Wasps. The 5-ATs were rather bigger and heavier than the earlier aircraft and had accommodation for thirteen to fifteen passengers compared with ten or eleven in the 4-ATs. The first few production aeroplanes had open cockpits, and later aircraft had cowled engines and spatted undercarriages. Some operated on twin-float and ski undercarriages.

A total of 194 Ford 4-AT and 5-AT monoplanes had been built when production ended in 1932 and they played an important part in the development of air transport in the United States. Twenty-three were operated by National Air Transport, nineteen by TWA, sixteen by Maddux Airlines, fourteen by American Airways, thirteen by Stout Air Services, twelve by Transcontinental Air Transport, eleven by Pan American Airways and nine by

Panagra. Many Tri-motors were exported, and during 1942–47 TACA in Nicaragua had sixteen, several came to the United Kingdom, some were used in Spain and four were used in New Guinea.

In November 1929 a Ford 4-AT made the first ever flight over the South Pole. This particular aircraft is in the Ford Museum at Dearborn, several others have been preserved and some may still be flying – eleven were known to be airworthy in September 1957, nearly 31 years after the first one entered service.

The slab-sided Fords and Fokkers as well as the host of fabric-covered biplanes gave good service to the American airlines but developments at Seattle, headquarters of Boeing, were to force their withdrawal from the main air routes. Boeing produced some very clean metal-skinned monoplanes with retractable undercarriages and from these evolved the Model 247 twin-engined ten-passenger transport with cantilever low-wing, smooth metal skin and retractable mainwheels. The first example flew on 8 February 1933, and United Air Lines placed an order for sixty. A most important feature of the Boeing 247 was its ability to climb with full load if one engine failed. A disadvantage was the main wing spars passing through the bottom of the passenger cabin. Improved versions were the Models 247A and 247D which were faster and had greater

One of the sixty Boeing 247s ordered by United Air Lines.

range; all were powered by Pratt & Whitney Wasp engines.

The Boeing 247 was really the prototype of the modern airliner but only 75 were built because it in its turn could not compete with a superior product from California – the Douglas DC-2.

The DC-2 really came into existence because Boeing could not sell Model 247s to TWA when the airline needed them to replace Fokkers and Fords and Douglas responded to a TWA request for a new three-engined aircraft. The result was in fact a twin-engined aeroplane that could do a better job than one with three engines. The new Douglas was of similar layout to the Boeing 247 but had fourteen seats, better performance and flaps. The prototype, known as the DC-1, made its first flight on 1 July 1933, and it nearly ended in disaster because of carburettor trouble, but this was cured and the DC-1 was delivered to TWA. In February 1934 it set a US transcontinental record when it carried mail from Los Angeles to New York in 13 hr 4 min. From that original DC-1 has evolved the long line of successful Douglas transports up to the present DC-8, DC-9 and DC-10 jets.

TWA ordered twenty of the production DC-2s which were essentially similar to the DC-1 and they entered regular service with the airline in July 1934 as the most advanced transport aeroplanes flying anywhere in the world. One of the features responsible for the DC-2's success was the Hamilton Standard variable-pitch propellers* fitted to its 710 hp Wright Cyclone engines, these propellers giving it greatly improved performance and the best single-engined performance then achieved by a twin-engined aeroplane. In Europe the first DC-2 went to KLM Royal Dutch Airlines and in October 1934 it won the handicap section of the England–Australia air race, taking only a few hours longer to reach Melbourne than the specially-designed de Havilland 88 Comet racer which came first in the speed section. It is believed that 200 Douglas DC-2s were built and that 160 went into airline service. Civil production ceased in 1936.

In August 1934 Northwest Airlines introduced the Lockheed Model 10 Electra, a twin-engined ten-passenger low-wing monoplane with retract-able undercarriage and twin fins and rudders. This was an important aeroplane because it was the first Lockheed transport of all-metal construction. There were several versions of the original Electra, 148 were built and most were powered by Pratt & Whitney Wasp Junior radial engines enclosed in neat cowlings. They were operated by a number of US airlines including Braniff, Chicago and Southern, Continental, and Pan American, and were used in Latin America, Europe, Australia and New Zealand. British Airways employed a fleet of seven on high-speed European services. Developments of the Electra were the Lockheed 14, Lodestar and war-time Hudson.

Although they did not play a vital part in air transport, mention should be made of the Electra's ancestors. These were a series of wooden aeroplanes with beautifully streamlined circular-section fuselages and broad wings. The first was the high-wing Vega which flew in 1927 and this was followed in 1928 by the parasol-wing Air Express which was designed for Western Air Express. In 1929 Lockheed built the low-wing Sirius seaplane for Charles Lindbergh and then in 1930 came a landplane development, the Orion. The Orion, which could carry four passengers, was the first commercial aeroplane with a retractable undercarriage, and with a 575 hp Wright Cyclone engine it could cruise at 180 mph.

* The variable-pitch propeller is one in which the angle of the blades can be varied to give maximum efficiency for take-off, climb and level flight.

One of the greatest aeroplanes ever built – the Douglas DC-3. ▶
It is seen here with the red markings of TWA.

Swissair used two on its Zürich–Munich–Vienna services, and it was the threat of Swissair's high-speed Orions which led to Germany building the Heinkel He 70 and Junkers-Ju 60/160 single-engined monoplanes.

This chapter closes with a description of one of the greatest and most important transport aeroplanes ever produced – the Douglas DC-3. American Airlines was operating its Condor biplanes on transcontinental sleeper services and these could not compete with the sleek Boeing 247 and Douglas DC-2 all-metal monoplanes. So American had to re-equip. The DC-2 fuselage was too narrow to provide space for sleeping berths, and to meet American's requirement Douglas designed the DST (Douglas Sleeper Transport). This was a scaled-up DC-2 with essentially the same structure but increased span and length and wider fuselage.

The prototype flew on 17 December 1935, and proved a great success. Its greater fuselage width allowed it to be operated with fourteen sleeping berths (DST) or 21 seats (DC-3) and both versions were put into production. American Airlines was the first to operate the DC-3, which it introduced on nonstop New York–Chicago services in June 1936, and the DST began transcontinental service on 18 September 1936, with a 17 hr 45 min westbound and 16 hr eastbound schedule.

The first DSTs and DC-3s were each powered by two 1,000 hp Wright Cyclone engines but 1,200 hp Pratt & Whitney Twin Wasps were soon used and a major proportion of the DC-3 series was powered by the latter engines. The aircraft were all equipped with variable-pitch propellers, autopilots and duplicated instrument panels and most had rubber-boot leading-edge wing and tail de-icing equipment.

By the time the United States entered the war in December 1941, more than 800 DC-3s had been produced of which some 450 were sold to airlines and these included 38 DSTs. Almost every major airline in the world has owned and operated DC-3s as have most of the air forces, and total production was close to 11,000. Massive wartime production took place of military DC-3s, including C-47s and C-53s (Dakotas) and large numbers of these were used after the war by airlines throughout the world. In the Soviet Union DC-3s were built under licence as PS-84s (later Lisunov Li-2s) and others were built in Japan.

DC-3s have been used for every conceivable type of transport work. They have been used for air dropping of troops and supplies, have worked as glider tugs and been operated on floats and skis. A number have even been fitted with propeller-turbines for engine development and research work. At least one DC-3 was converted to a glider.

No other single type of aeroplane has made such a tremendous contribution to the development of air transport or brought air transport to so many widely differing types of community throughout the world. At the end of 1974 there were still nearly 600 DC-3s in airline service, excluding unknown numbers in the Soviet Union, and one aircraft in the United States is known to have flown in excess of 84,000 hr. One Eastern Air Lines DC-3 has been preserved in the Smithsonian Institution, Washington.

	Span	Length	Passengers	Loaded weight	Cruising speed	Range
Ford 4-AT Tri-motor	74′ 0″	49′ 10″	10/11	10,000 lb	107 mph	580 miles
Boeing Model 40A	44′ 2¼″	33′ 2¼″	2	6,000 lb	105 mph	650 miles
Boeing Model 80	80′ 0″	54′ 11″	12	15,276 lb	115 mph	545 miles
Curtiss Condor Model 18	91′ 8″	57′ 6″	18	17,900 lb	118 mph	810 miles
Fokker F-32	99′ 0″	70′ 2″	32	22,500 lb	123 mph	530 miles
Boeing Model 247	74′ 0″	51′ 4″	10	12,650 lb	155 mph	485 miles
Douglas DC-2	85′ 0″	62′ 0″	14	18,080 lb	170 mph	1,193 miles
Lockheed Model 10 Electra	55′ 0″	38′ 7″	10	10,500 lb	180 mph	810 miles
Douglas DC-3	95′ 0″	64′ 6″	21	25,200 lb	180 mph	1,500 miles

9

British Monoplanes

Britain was slow to adopt the monoplane as a transport aircraft, and as late as 1934 Imperial Airways, the national airline, actually commissioned two large and several smaller four-engined biplanes. However, a step in the right direction had taken place early in 1933 when a fleet of Armstrong Whitworth XV Atalanta four-engined high-wing cantilever monoplanes began operating the Kisumu–Cape Town section of the England–South Africa route.

The first Atalanta made its maiden flight in June 1932, eight were built and the type was used to operate the southern part of the South Africa route and to develop the eastern route beyond Karachi, eventually to Singapore. The structure was mainly of metal with plywood and fabric covering and the engines were four 340 hp Armstrong Siddeley Serval

III air-cooled radials driving two-blade wooden propellers. Normal passenger accommodation was nine to eleven and there was a large forward mail compartment.

Imperial Airways' next important monoplanes were the Short C class flying-boats, but two other important land monoplanes were introduced into service before the 1939–45 war. One of these was another Armstrong Whitworth design, the A.W.27 Ensign, and the other the beautiful all-wood de Havilland 91 Albatross.

The Ensign was a large high-wing monoplane, mostly of metal construction, with a vast retractable undercarriage. Two versions were built, a forty-passenger aircraft for European routes and a 27-passenger type for the Empire routes. Fourteen were built, the first one flew in January 1938 and the type

The *Athena*, one of Imperial Airways' Armstrong Whitworth Atalanta monoplanes, seen at Karachi.

began to work European services at the end of that year, but various troubles prevented their full introduction before the war and the fleet passed to BOAC in 1940. Originally the engines were four 850 hp Armstrong Siddeley Tiger IXs but these gave trouble and eventually 950 hp Wright Cyclones were fitted. An unusual feature at that time was provision of a smoking cabin. It was planned that the Empire version would have twenty sleeping berths but these were never fitted.

The Albatross was one of the most beautiful British aircraft ever built. It had a finely stream-lined circular-section fuselage, tapered wing and twin fins and rudders; the undercarriage retracted inwards, and the four 525 hp de Havilland Gipsy Twelve engines were enclosed in very neat cowlings with pointed spinners. The structure was entirely of wood and the fuselage was a moulded sandwich of plywood with balsa filling. Five 21-passenger aircraft were built for Imperial Airways' European routes and operated under the class name Frobisher and there were two long-range examples intended

The beautiful de Havilland Albatross – this was one of the two long-range mailplanes built for the Air Ministry.

for North Atlantic mail operations. The passenger aircraft entered service late in 1938 but their full commercial potential was cut short by the war. *Frobisher* flew from Croydon to Paris in 53 min in

November 1938, and in January 1939 another aircraft, *Falcon*, flew from Croydon to Brussels in 48 min and from Croydon to Marseilles in 3 hr.

Of very different design was the de Havilland 95

Flamingo. This was a twin-engined metal high-wing monoplane with retractable undercarriage. It was powered by 930 hp Bristol Perseus XVI engines and could carry twelve to seventeen passengers. One was used by Jersey Airways in 1939 and the other fifteen served with BOAC and the Royal Navy.

By agreement with the United States, Britain was not to build transport aircraft during the war, using instead its full production facilities for operational military aircraft, but in spite of this Avro did develop a transport version of its four-engined Lancaster bomber and towards the end of the war some Lancasters were converted on the production line for transport duties – these types were respectively the York and the Lancastrian.

The Lancaster bomber was an all-metal mid-wing monoplane with twin fins and rudders and retractable main undercarriage. Most were powered by four Rolls-Royce Merlin liquid-cooled engines. The York employed the same wing, engine installation and tail unit as the Lancaster but had a larger square-section fuselage, a central fin, and the wing was mounted in the high position. The Merlins used were each of 1,620 hp.

The first Yorks were supplied to the Royal Air Force and one, named *Ascalon*, was used by Winston Churchill and by HM King George VI. Five early production aircraft went to BOAC as mixed passenger-cargo aircraft and they entered service on 22 April 1944, on the United Kingdom–Gibraltar–Tripoli–Cairo route. A total of 257 Yorks was built including one built by Victory Aircraft in Canada.

BOAC acquired more Yorks after the war and finally withdrew them from passenger service in October 1950. The type was also used by British South American Airways (BSAA), South African Airways, FAMA in the Argentine, Middle East Airlines, and numerous independent airlines and charter companies in Britain, Canada and South Africa. RAF Yorks made an important contribution to the Berlin Airlift in 1948–49 and three were used on this operation by Skyways. Although a wartime conversion of a bomber, the York gave good service but was abominably noisy both inside and out.

The Lancastrian was simply a Lancaster with military equipment removed, a faired-in nose and tail, and a passenger cabin. BOAC and BSAA (British South American Airways) both had fleets of Lancastrians and they were used by Qantas, Trans-Canada Air Lines and Alitalia. A joint BOAC–Qantas United Kingdom–Australia service was begun with Lancastrians in May 1945 and a few weeks later the service was speeded up to give a journey time of only 63 hr. The Lancastrian was also the first British aeroplane to operate across the

South Atlantic when BSAA began London–Buenos Aires services in March 1946.

Another bomber conversion was the Handley Page Halton. This was a civil version of the Handley Page Halifax four-engined bomber. It was powered by 1,675 hp Bristol Hercules 100 air-cooled radial engines, had ten passenger seats and, beneath the fuselage, a cargo pannier. BOAC had a fleet of twelve Haltons, introduced them on London–Cairo services on 9 September 1946, and to Karachi and Colombo in 1947, but mostly used them on services to West Africa. Numbers of Haltons were used by British private operators and 41 were used on the Berlin Airlift.

On 2 December 1945 a completely new British transport aeroplane made its first flight. This was the Bristol Type 170 twin-engined high-wing monoplane. It was an ugly aeroplane with deep slab-sided fuselage and non-retractable undercarriage and was produced in two main versions, as the Wayfarer with 32 seats and the Freighter with nose-loading doors. Eventually 214 Bristol 170s were built and there were seventeen variants including the lengthened Mk. 32 Superfreighter. Bristol Hercules sleeve-valve radial engines of 1,675–1,980 hp were used in the various Type 170 models.

In June 1964 Channel Islands Airways began using the prototype Wayfarer on its services to the Channel Islands; but the Bristol 170 will best be remembered for the years of service it gave on Silver City Airways' cross-Channel vehicle ferry routes, and the Mk. 32 was actually developed at Silver City's request. The vehicle ferry version of the standard Freighter could carry two cars in the hold and aft of this was a cabin for sixteen passengers, but the Mk. 32 Superfreighter could carry three medium-sized cars and 23 passengers.

Bristol Freighters were also used by Straits Air Freight Express of New Zealand for ferry services linking North and South Island, they were used by Australian National Airways for the carriage of beef, and by numerous other airlines and air forces. Wayfarers were used by Indian National Airways, West African Airways and other operators in many parts of the world.

Air Charter operated Superfreighters on vehicle ferry services from Southend from 1955 and later the fleets of Air Charter and Silver City were merged and operated under the title British United Air Ferries. A sixty-passenger version, known as the Super-Wayfarer was operated on the air sector of Silver City's London–Paris coach-air service.

It was also in 1946 that another important British transport aeroplane entered service. This was the Vickers-Armstrongs Viking which made its first flight on 22 June 1945. The Viking was a twin-engined mid-wing monoplane with single fin and rudder and retractable undercarriage. It comprised an oval-section all-metal fuselage married to the fabric-covered metal wing of the Wellington bomber, but later versions had new metal-skinned wings. For several years Vikings, at first with 21 seats, later with 27 and eventually with 36, formed the backbone of the British European Airways fleet. They entered service on 1 September 1946 on the Northolt–Copenhagen service and were later used on BEA services extending from Scandinavia to Cairo. The engines were 1,675/1,690 hp Bristol Hercules radials.

A total of 163 Vikings was built and the airlines they served included Aer Lingus, Air-India, British West Indian Airways, Central African Airways, Danish Air Lines, Indian National Airways, Indian Airlines Corporation (IAC), Iraqi Airways, Misrair and South African Airways and many independent companies including Airwork, BKS, Eagle and Hunting.

One Viking was temporarily fitted with two Rolls-Royce Nene turbojets, thus making it the world's first jet-powered transport but it did not go into airline service. Similar to the Viking was the military Valetta of which 263 were built.

As early as 1943 it was realised that once the war ended BOAC would require aircraft capable of operating over the North Atlantic, and designs were prepared for what was to become the Avro Tudor 1, a low-wing monoplane with accommodation for 12–28 passengers. It was powered by four 1,750 hp Rolls-Royce Merlin liquid-cooled engines and was the first British production aeroplane with a pressurised cabin. Twenty were ordered for BOAC, the prototype flew in June 1945, and one was named *Elizabeth of England* in a ceremony at London Airport. A much lengthened version, the Tudor 2, was also ordered for BOAC's Commonwealth routes but due to serious shortcomings in the aircraft and changing requirements of BOAC, the corporation never operated a Tudor.

Four of the Tudor 1s were completed as slightly lengthened Tudor 4s for BSAA and two of the completed Tudor 1s were modified for the same airline as Tudor 4Bs. These had accommodation for 32 and 28 passengers respectively. At the end of October 1947 BSAA began operating Tudors on a London–Lisbon–Azores–Bermuda–Nassau–Havana service, and in December 1948 Tudors started working right down the west coast of South America and thence across the Andes to Buenos Aires. In January 1948 the Tudor *Star Tiger* had disappeared in the west Atlantic with 31 passengers and crew aboard and then a year later *Star Ariel* was lost between Bermuda and Jamaica with twenty aboard. No wreckage of either aircraft was discovered, the type was grounded and its failure led to the absorption of BSAA by BOAC.

A number of the surviving Tudor 1s and 4s were later drastically modified by Aviation Traders and put into service as Super Traders by Air Charter. Some Tudors did useful work on the Berlin Airlift, one Tudor 1 became the Tudor 8 with four Rolls-Royce Nene turbojets and six Tudor 2s became jet-powered Ashtons for research work.

Another transport built for BOAC was the Handley Page Hermes, a four-engined low-wing monoplane. The prototype crashed and was destroyed on its first flight on 2 December 1945, but modified production aircraft entered service with the RAF as the Hastings. From this was developed the pressurised and lengthened Hermes 4 which had a retractable nosewheel undercarriage. It was powered by four 2,100 hp Bristol Hercules engines and initially had accommodation for forty passengers. Twenty-four Hermes 4s were built for BOAC and they began working African services in November 1950. Some of these aircraft passed to British independent airlines and they were also used by Bahamas Airways, Kuwait Airways and Middle East Airlines.

Last of the major piston-engined British transport monoplanes to enter service was the Airspeed A.S.57

Ambassador. This was a good looking all-metal twin-engined high-wing monoplane with pressurised cabin, finely tapered wing, retractable nosewheel undercarriage and triple fins. It was powered, in production form, by two 2,700 hp Bristol Centaurus 661 radial engines and the prototype first flew on 10 July 1947.

BEA had a fleet of twenty Ambassadors, they began service in March 1952 under the class name Elizabethan, and the type was retired at the end of July 1958 after flying 31 mn miles and carrying 2,430,000 passengers. They then began a new career with British independent airlines, including Autair, BKS Air Transport and Dan-Air. Three were used in Australia by Butler Air Transport, some were used by Globe Air of Switzerland and one was acquired by the King of Morocco. A number of British-operated Ambassadors were converted to cargo carriers and at least one was employed by BKS Air Transport as a flying horsebox. The second prototype and the production prototype were both fitted for periods with propeller-turbines for experimental purposes. The former flew with Bristol Proteus, Rolls-Royce Tyne and Dart turbines and the latter had Napier Elands.

Although it never went into service, one other British transport monoplane must be mentioned. It was the Bristol 167 Brabazon designed for non-

An Airspeed Ambassador – the last piston-engined major British airliner.

stop operation between London and New York. It was a very large aeroplane with a span of 230 ft and a loaded weight of 290,000 lb. Its eight 2,500 hp Bristol Centaurus engines were buried in the wing and coupled in pairs to drive four contra-rotating propellers. This large aeroplane made its first flight on 4 September 1949, but it flew for less than 400 hr and was broken up in 1953 without ever going into service. The production version would have had Coupled-Proteus propeller-turbines and accommodation for up to a hundred passengers. The Brabazon was the biggest, although not the heaviest, landplane ever built in Britain. Although never used, the Brabazon did contribute to technical experience.

	Span		Length		Passengers	Loaded weight	Cruising speed	Range
Armstrong Whitworth Atalanta	90′	0″	71′	6″	9/11	21,000 lb	130 mph	400 miles
Armstrong Whitworth Ensign	123′	0″	114′	0″	27/40	49,000 lb	170 mph	800 miles
de Havilland Albatross	105′	0″	71′	6″	21	29,500 lb	210 mph	1,040 miles
de Havilland Flamingo	70′	0″	51′	2″	12/17	17,600 lb	184 mph	1,210 miles
Avro York	102′	0″	78′	6″	21/54	68,000 lb	233 mph	2,700 miles
Bristol Wayfarer	108′	0″	68′	4″	20/54	40,000 lb	163 mph	900 miles
Vickers-Armstrongs Viking	89′	3″	65′	2″	21/36	34,000 lb	210 mph	1,700 miles
Avro Tudor 4	120′	0″	85′	3″	32	80,000 lb	210 mph	4,000 miles
Handley Page Hermes 4	113′	0″	96′	10″	40/56	86,000 lb	276 mph	2,000 miles
Airspeed Ambassador	115′	0″	81′	0″	47/55	52,500 lb	260 mph	550 miles

10

The Great Americans

This chapter is concerned with the fleets of twin- and four-engined all-metal low-wing monoplanes designed and built in the United States and which carried a large proportion of the world's air traffic between the end of the 1939–45 war and the introduction of jet airliners from 1958. These aircraft include the types which made possible regular North Atlantic services and, later, nonstop US transcontinental and North Atlantic services.

Because many of these aircraft formed families stemming from a basic type they are not described here in chronological sequence.

The first of the American four-engined monoplanes to enter airline service was the Boeing 307 Stratoliner. Although only ten Stratoliners were built they hold an important place in aviation history as the first airliners with pressure cabins. The Stratoliner was developed from the famous B-17 Flying Fortress bomber and employed B-17 wings, engines, nacelles and, in original form, tail unit, combined with a new circular-section pressurised fuselage. The engines were 900 hp Wright Cyclones, and standard passenger accommodation was for 33. TWA had a fleet of five Stratoliners and introduced them on 8 July 1940, on the transcontinental route and in the same month put them on New York–Boston services. Pan American Airways had three Stratoliners on Latin American routes. In 1941 the Stratoliners were called up for military service, including a North Atlantic operation from April 1942, but after the war the TWA aircraft were rebuilt as unpressurised 38-passenger aircraft and put back into civil operation. Subsequently Stratoliners were used in Central America, by the

French company Aigle Azur and by companies in the Far East.

In mid-1935 the five major US airlines began discussing with Douglas their requirements for a large four-engined trunk route aeroplane and a prototype was constructed as the 52-passenger pressurised DC-4E which flew on 7 June 1938. However, the aircraft was not successful and a scaled-down unpressurised version was put into production as the DC-4. Sixty-one DC-4s were ordered by American Airlines, Eastern Air Lines and United Air Lines, but by the time the first aircraft flew, on 14 February 1942, the United States was at war and all the DC-4s were taken over by the air force as C-54 Skymasters. A total of 1,163 Skymasters was built and many of these, as well as 79 post-war DC-4s, were used by airlines when peace returned.

American Airlines was first to introduce DC-4s into domestic operation when on 7 March 1946 they began working between New York and Los Angeles. American Overseas Airlines had put DC-4s into transatlantic service at the end of October 1945 when the first New York–Hurn (for London) service was flown, with two stops, in 23 hr 48 min. Eventually DC-4s were used by airlines all over the world. Initially DC-4s had 44 seats but later, high-density versions carried as many as 86 passengers. The

engines were four 1,450 hp Pratt & Whitney R-2000s.

An interesting development of the DC-4 was the Carvair conversion made in Britain in 1961. In this type the flight deck was raised above the cabin and nose doors were fitted for the loading of vehicles – six cars and 22 passengers could be carried. About twenty Carvair conversions were made.

Even before the DC-4 began commercial service within the United States the Lockheed Constellation had been put on the transcontinental route by TWA, and the DC-4 was at a disadvantage competing against the pressurised and faster Lockheed product. So Douglas built an enlarged and pressurised development of the DC-4 with better performance. This was the DC-6 for which substantial initial orders were placed by American Airlines and United Air Lines. Both airlines introduced the type on 27 April 1946, American on the New York–Chicago route and United on the transcontinental route with an eastbound journey time of about 10 hr. DC-6s were used by many major airlines and over 170 were built. These aircraft had four 2,400 hp Pratt & Whitney R-2800 engines and originally had accommodation for fifty passengers.

After the DC-6 came the DC-6A cargo and DC-6B passenger developments which had longer fuselages

One of the fleet of Douglas DC-6s used by United Air Lines under the title *Mainliner 300*.

and increased range. Most of the DC-6As were used by the US Air Force and Navy but the DC-6B found favour with the world's airlines and 288 were built. American Airlines introduced the DC-6B on transcontinental services on 29 April 1951, and the type remained in production until 1958. These aircraft started life as 54-seaters but high-density seating was later provided for up to 102 passengers.

The DC-6B proved to be one of the most reliable and economic transport aeroplanes ever built and it ranks in history alongside the DC-3 as one of the world's great aeroplanes.

Production of the 3,250 hp Curtiss-Wright Turbo-Compound engine enabled Douglas to produce a heavier and longer-range aeroplane than the DC-6B and one with nonstop US transcontinental capability. This was the 60/95-passenger DC-7 and it was put into service by American Airlines on nonstop New York–Los Angeles services on 29 November 1953. It worked to an 8 hr eastbound schedule and 8 hr 45 min westbound. Only American Airlines, Delta Air Lines, National Airlines and United Air Lines bought DC-7s and 110 were built. Some were later converted to DC-7F cargo carriers.

The DC-7B was designed as a longer-range version of the basic DC-7 and many of them had saddle fuel tanks in extended engine nacelles. They entered service in 1955, 112 were built and all were employed by United States airlines except for four supplied to South African Airways.

Last of the Douglas piston-engined airliners was the DC-7C Seven Seas designed to meet Pan American World Airways' requirements for an aeroplane capable of nonstop operation in both directions across the North Atlantic and at the same time having a lower interior noise level than the

DC-7B. The wing span was increased by 10 ft to 127 ft 6 in and this increased fuel capacity and put the 3,400 hp Turbo-Compound engines 5 ft further out from the fuselage than the engines in the earlier DC-7s. The fuselage was also lengthened, by 3 ft 4 in, and accommodation ranged from sixty in first-class seating to 105 in a high-density layout.

Pan American introduced DC-7Cs on the North Atlantic route on 1 June 1956, and BOAC began using them on the London–New York *Monarch* service in January 1957. SAS (Scandinavian Airlines System) began a Polar service with DC-7Cs on 24 February 1957 between Copenhagen and Tokyo via Anchorage in Alaska. Other DC-7C operators included Alitalia, Braniff International Airways, CMA of Mexico, Japan Air Lines, KLM, Northwest Airlines, Sabena, Swissair, and TAI of France. A total of 121 Seven Seas were built and numbers of them were converted into freighters as they were replaced on passenger service by jets.

An interesting development of the Douglas four-engined transports was built in Montreal by Canadair. This was the Canadair Four produced in several versions. The first was essentially a DC-4 with Rolls-Royce Merlin liquid-cooled engines, then came the pressurised DC-4M-2, DC-4M-4 and C-4 which were really Merlin-powered DC-6s with shortened fuselages. Canadair Fours formed the main fleet of

Trans-Canada Air Lines (now Air Canada) for several years, they served with Canadian Pacific Air Lines on trans-Pacific routes and, as the Argonaut class, operated many BOAC routes from 1949 until 1960 during which time they flew nearly 107 mn miles and carried 870,000 passengers. It was the Canadair Four *Atalanta* which carried HM Queen Elizabeth II from Entebbe in Uganda to London on the day of her accession to the Throne.

Another outstanding family of United States transport aeroplanes was Lockheed's series of Constellations and Super Constellations. The original L-049 Constellation was designed to meet a 1939 requirement of TWA for a long-range four-engined aeroplane. It was of about the same size as the Douglas DC-4 but of more advanced aerodynamic design with finely-shaped fuselage and triple fins and rudders, and, most important, the fuselage was pressurised. When the prototype flew in January 1943 it proved to be about 100 mph faster than contemporary transports.

TWA and Pan American Airways both ordered fleets of Constellations but they were taken over by the USAF as C-69s and the first went into service in April 1944. At the end of the war civil Constellations were produced and most of the military C-69s were sold to airlines. Civil operation began on 3 February 1946, when Pan American intro-

duced Constellations on the New York–Bermuda route and in the same month TWA began flying the type between Washington and Paris and New York and Los Angeles. The first purely civil Constellation was the L-649 and it was followed by the improved L-649A, L-749 and L-749A. All were powered by Wright Cyclone R-3350 engines of from 2,200 to 2,500 hp. Passenger accommodation ranged from 44 first class to 81 in high-density seating and some aircraft could be fitted with under-fuselage removable 'Speedpaks' capable of carrying nearly four tons of cargo.

Lockheed built 233 Constellations, including military and naval versions, and they were used by most major United States airlines and a number of European airlines. They also served Air-India, South African Airways and Qantas.

In 1950, following discussions with Eastern Air Lines, Lockheed developed the Constellation design still further by lengthening the fuselage by more than 18 ft and fitting 2,700 hp Cyclones. Known as the L-1049 Super Constellation, this version entered service with Eastern at the end of 1951. Passenger accommodation was 66 first class or up to 102 in high-density. Further development, with the use of 3,400 hp Wright Turbo-Compound engines, led through the L-1049C, D and E models to the final L-1049G (passenger) and L-1049H (passenger/

cargo) which had take-off weights nearly double that of the original Constellation although all versions used the same basic wing. The L-1049G and H models could be fitted with large streamlined wingtip fuel tanks.

More than 600 Super Constellations were built and they served many of the world's major airlines as well as the US Air Force and Navy. The Constellation and Super Constellation played a major part in the development of long-distance air services and a few are still in service.

Finally Lockheed undertook major redesign of the Super Constellation to meet the competition from the long-range Douglas DC-7C. This was the L-1649A Starliner which retained the Super Constellation fuselage but had a completely new one-piece thin-wing of 150 ft span. With a maximum-fuel range of more than 6,000 miles and seating for up to 99 passengers, the Turbo-Compound engined L-1649A was a magnificent aeroplane, but, only coming into service on 1 June 1957, when TWA put them on nonstop New York–London services, the aircraft was too late to attract orders because the turbine-powered transports were soon to enter service. This late appearance limited production to 43 and they were only operated new by TWA, Air France and Lufthansa.

Douglas and Lockheed four-engined transports carried the bulk of the world's long-distance air traffic from the end of the 1939–45 war until the large-scale introduction of jet aircraft around 1960, but there was one other United States aircraft which played an important rôle. This was the Boeing 377 Stratocruiser which entered service over the North Atlantic with Pan American in 1949.

The Stratocruiser was a civil version of the C-97 military transport, which in turn was a development of the B-29 and B-50 Superfortresses, and the airliner used the same wings, engine installation and tail unit as the B-50. Unlike the Douglas and Lockheed aircraft, the Stratocruiser was a mid-wing monoplane and it had a double-bubble double-deck fuselage with blunt nose and upswept rear. The main deck had seating for 55–100 passengers and on the lower deck was the cargo hold and a lounge and bar with seats for up to fourteen, the lounge being connected to the main deck by a circular stairway. The Stratocruiser was popular with passengers, particularly on the first class BOAC *Monarch* and Pan American *President* New York–London services, and with crews, who liked its spacious flight deck and unobstructed view.

Although 888 Boeing C-97 series aircraft were built there were only 55 civil Stratocruisers – the initial orders being twenty Pan American, four SAS, eight American Overseas Airlines, ten North-

◄ *Lawrence Hargrave*, seen here, was one of the fleet of Lockheed L-749 Constellations used by Qantas Empire Airways.

west Airlines, six BOAC and seven United Air Lines. SAS never took delivery and their aircraft passed to BOAC which eventually operated seventeen, and the AOA aircraft passed to Pan American. Stratocruisers remained on the North Atlantic until replaced in 1958 by de Havilland Comet 4s and Boeing 707-121s. After their mainline service Stratocruisers passed to various operators including Transocean Airlines which modified some to carry 117 passengers. A number of Stratocruisers were converted by Aero Spacelines to the Guppy series with very large-diameter fuselages for the carriage of spacecraft sections and other bulky loads.

The engines used to power the Stratocruisers were four 3,500 hp Pratt & Whitney Double Wasps.

For short-stage services Convair produced an outstanding family of twin-engined low-wing monoplanes and Martin built two types of similar layout.

The Convair series began with the CV-240 Convair-Liner which first flew in March 1947 and entered service on 1 June 1948, with American Airlines. In initial configuration the CV-240 had seats for forty passengers and it quickly gained favour as a DC-3 replacement with many airlines in the United States; with KLM, Sabena and Swissair in Europe; with Trans-Australia Airlines, Garuda Indonesian Airways, Ethiopian Airlines and with the Chinese Central Air Transport. A

total of 176 civil and 395 military CV-240s was built. The engines were 2,400 hp Pratt & Whitney R-2800 air-cooled radials. The CV-240 and subsequent models had pressurised cabins and retractable nosewheel undercarriages and some had ventral airstairs (passenger steps).

In 1952 an improved Convair-Liner entered service; this was the more powerful CV-340 with increased span and lengthened fuselage to take an extra seat row. Convair built 209 civil CV-340s and 108 military examples and the type was used by several US airlines. Outside the USA operators included Alitalia, Finnair, Garuda, JAT of Yugoslavia, KLM, Lufthansa, Philippine Air Lines, Saudi Arabian Airlines and a number of airlines in South America.

The final model was the CV-440 Metropolitan which could carry up to 56 passengers and incorporated a number of modifications mostly aimed at reducing cabin noise. Powered by 2,500 hp R-2800 engines, the Metropolitan entered service in February 1956 with Continental Airlines, and many of the earlier Convair operators adopted the type or modified their CV-340s to CV-440 standard. With the introduction of the Metropolitan SAS and Iberia joined the ranks of Convair operators.

After many years of outstanding service numbers of Convair-Liners were converted to turbine power,

One of Finnair's blue and white Convair CV-440 Metropolitans.

as described in the next chapter.

The Martin twin-engined monoplanes did not enjoy the same success as the Convairs. The first of them, the Martin 2-0-2, was a 42-passenger unpressurised aircraft which entered service in November 1947 with Northwest Airlines in the United States and LAN in Chile. The engines were Pratt & Whitney R-2800s and the Martin 2-0-2, like the Convairs, had a retractable nosewheel undercarriage. One of NWA's aircraft had a wing failure in flight and all 2-0-2s were withdrawn from service, a number of orders were cancelled and only 33 were built.

A modified version, the 2-0-2A, appeared in 1950 and twelve were built for TWA while some of the 2-0-2s were brought to this standard. Most were used by various US local service airlines as were ten of the TWA aircraft.

The final version of the Martin was the pressurised 4-0-4 which entered service with TWA in October 1951. This version had 2,400 hp Pratt & Whitney R-2800 engines and seats for up to 48 tourist class passengers or 52 in high-density.

The prototype 4-0-4 was a rebuilt 2-0-2, 41 new aircraft were produced for TWA, sixty for Eastern Air Lines and two for the US Coast Guard to give a total of 104. Eventually most passed to local service operators.

	Span		Length		Passengers	Loaded weight	Cruising speed	Range
Boeing Stratoliner	107′	3″	74′	4″	33/38	42,000 lb	220 mph	2,390 miles
Douglas DC-4	117′	6″	93′	11″	44/86	73,000 lb	219 mph	4,420 miles
Lockheed L-749	123′	0″	95′	2″	44/81	105,000 lb	298 mph	1,760 miles
Convair CV-240	91′	9″	74′	8″	40	42,400 lb	235 mph	1,300 miles
Boeing Stratocruiser	141′	3″	110′	4″	55/117	148,000 lb	340 mph	4,200 miles
Douglas DC-6B	117′	6″	105′	7″	54/102	107,000 lb	315 mph	3,005 miles
Martin 4-0-4	93′	3½″	74′	7″	40/52	44,900 lb	276 mph	1,070 miles
Lockheed L-1049G	123′	0″	113′	7″	63/99	137,500 lb	355 mph	3,070 miles
Douglas DC-7C	127′	6″	112′	3″	60/105	143,000 lb	354 mph	4,606 miles

11

Propeller-turbine Power

During the 1939–45 war Britain became the leader in the development of the gas-turbine engine and when design began of the post-war generation of transport aeroplanes the British aircraft industry was the first to exploit the turbine as a means of propulsion for commercial aircraft. The speed advantages of the turbojet or pure-jet were fully realised but these power units were not considered suitable for short-range aircraft at that time; instead it was decided to use turbines to drive propellers, and a transport aircraft using this system was designed by Vickers-Armstrongs.

This first propeller-turbine transport was the Viscount which proved to be the most successful major British transport aircraft ever produced, with a total of 445 built. More than sixty operators in about forty countries placed orders for Viscounts, and North American orders alone brought in more than £58 mn.

The Viscount was a pressurised all-metal low-wing monoplane with retractable nosewheel undercarriage. It was of orthodox design but the feature which brought about its success was its four Rolls-Royce Dart propeller-turbines.

The first example was the V.630 with seats for 32 passengers and engines each of 1,380 hp. This aircraft flew for the first time on 16 July 1948, and on 29 July 1950 it flew from London to Paris, operating the first air service ever flown by a turbine-powered aeroplane. It remained on the Paris route for two weeks with BEA and then for a short period operated the airline's London–Edinburgh service, but it did not go into regular service because it was too small to be economic.

Instead, BEA ordered a fleet of V.701 Viscounts with 1,547 hp Darts and seats for 47 passengers. This type went into service on 18 April 1953 on BEA's services to the Eastern Mediterranean, and Viscounts of various models have been in constant service ever since. The Viscount was the first British transport aeroplane to be ordered in quantity by airlines in the United States.

Nearly 300 Viscount 700 series aircraft were built and they offered new standards of comfort on all the routes they served and brought about a rapid increase in traffic.

Further development produced the series 800 and 810 Viscounts with engines of up to 1,990 hp and accommodation for up to 65 passengers with, later, high-density seating for 77.

BEA operated a total of 73 Viscounts, Capital Airlines in the USA had sixty of which nearly fifty passed to United Air Lines, and Trans-Canada Air Lines had 51. Aer Lingus, Air France, Alitalia, All Nippon Airways, Ansett-ANA, Continental Airlines, Indian Airlines Corporation, Lufthansa, New Zealand National, Pakistan International, South African Airways, Trans-Australia Airlines and many others including CAAC, the Chinese State airline, had Viscount fleets and about 130 are still in airline service.

The second British propeller-turbine transport

The first propeller-turbine airliner to enter service – one of BEA's Vickers-Armstrongs Viscount V.701s.

to enter service was the Bristol 175 Britannia. This was originally conceived as a piston-engined aircraft for BOAC's medium-range Empire routes but was built as a turbine-powered aircraft with four Bristol Proteus engines. The Britannia was a large low-wing monoplane and first flew on 16 August 1952, but its development programme was prolonged, partly because of engine problems, and it did not enter service until 1 February 1957, when BOAC introduced the type on the London–Johannesburg route. This first version was the Britannia 102 with 3,900 hp Proteus engines and accommodation for up to ninety passengers.

From the original aeroplane the longer-range series 300 and 310 Britannias were developed. These had 4,120 hp engines, were 10 ft 3 in longer and capable of operating nonstop in each direction over the North Atlantic. In high-density layout they could carry 139 passengers. BOAC operated the first North Atlantic service to be flown by a turbine-powered aeroplane when it introduced Britannia 312s on the London–New York route on 19 December 1957. On the same day an El Al Britannia made a nonstop proving flight of 6,100 miles from New York to Tel Aviv at an average speed of 401 mph.

The Britannia was a superb aeroplane but it appeared too late and only 85 were built including prototypes and 23 of the series 250 aircraft for the Royal Air Force. Apart from BOAC and El Al, its civil operators included Aeronaves de Mexico, Canadian Pacific Air Lines, Cubana, Ghana Airways and Transcontinental SA of the Argentine. Later, many Britannias passed to British independent airlines.

The next British propeller-turbine airliner to go into service was the Vickers-Armstrongs Vanguard which was designed to meet the requirements of BEA and Trans-Canada Air Lines. This was a large mid-wing monoplane seating up to 139 passengers and powered by four 4,985/5,545 hp Rolls-Royce Tyne propeller-turbines. It had large lower deck cargo holds.

The Vanguard first flew on 20 January 1959, and began operation with BEA on 17 December 1960, with regular operation from March 1961, a month after TCA's introduction of the type.

Although it was an outstanding aeroplane giving good service, particularly on British domestic trunk routes, it was, like the Britannia, too late, and total production was 43 with all going to BEA and TCA. As Vanguards were replaced by jet aircraft both airlines began converting some of their fleets to freighters while others appeared on the second-hand market.

Britain also produced two propeller-turbine powered short-haul transports – the twin-engined Handley Page Herald and Avro (later Hawker Siddeley) 748. The Herald was a 38/50-passenger high-wing monoplane of promising design but it proved unable to compete with the very similar Fokker F.27 Friendship. It was originally designed to have four piston engines but was modified to have two Rolls-Royce Darts. The turbine version flew in March 1958 and entered service in May 1961. It was ordered in small quantities by operators in Europe, Canada, Jordan and Latin America but only 48 were sold.

The Avro 748, a low-wing monoplane with two Darts, has proved much more successful. The prototype flew in June 1960 and about 300 have been sold to civil and military operators, with about a quarter of these produced in India by the Kanpur Division of Hindustan Aeronautics for Indian Airlines Corporation and the Indian Air Force. Most Avro 748 orders have been for small batches, but Aerolineas Argentinas and Philippine Air Lines each ordered twelve and Varig of Brazil and the Royal Australian Air Force each acquired ten. Indian Airlines will possibly have a fleet of 22. Under the type name Andover the aircraft is in service with the Royal Air Force, two serving the Queen's Flight. In its latest form the 748 has two 2,280 hp Darts and can carry up to 62 passengers. Its take-off run is only 2,750 ft and it is frequently operated from rough dirt runways.

One of the most successful propeller-turbine transports is the Dutch Fokker F.27 Friendship which has outsold the Viscount by a considerable margin. In appearance the twin-engined high-wing Friendship is similar to the Herald but with more delicate lines. Fokker started out by fitting Dart engines and the rightness of the design is proved by the twenty years of continuous sales.

The Friendship has undergone continuous development since its appearance in November 1955,

A red and white Fokker F.27 Friendship of Balair.

the power of the Darts has been increased from 1,670 hp to 2,230 hp and seating from 32 to a maximum of 56. There are also freight, mixed passenger/cargo, mail, and troop-carrying versions. Apart from being built in Amsterdam, the type was built under licence in the United States by Fairchild (later Fairchild Hiller) where developed versions were the F-27J and FH-227.

By January 1975 a total of 138 operators in 54 countries had bought 629 Friendships. The largest number are used by airlines and as executive transports, and the rest have gone to air forces, civil aviation authorities, heads of State and the French Ministère des Postes et Télécommunications. The Ansett group of airlines in Australia bought 23; Trans-Australia Airlines nineteen; All Nippon Airways and Fujita Airlines in Japan 25; Ozark Airlines, Mohawk Airlines, Piedmont Airlines and Bonanza Airlines in the USA 25, 23, eighteen and thirteen respectively; Philippine Air Lines and Malaysia-Singapore Airlines each bought seventeen; Indian Airlines fifteen; Aero Trasporti Italiani fourteen; and Pakistan International Airlines fifteen. In France fifteen Friendships were used on the night mail services.

The Canadian company Canadair produced a number of developments of the Britannia. These included the CL-28 Argus with Turbo-Compound engines for the Royal Canadian Air Force and a series of Rolls-Royce Tyne propeller-turbine powered CL-44s for cargo and passenger transport. A number of CL-44Ds with lengthened fuselages and swing-tail rear loading were bought by cargo airlines and a few were supplied to the Icelandic airline Loftleidir for cheap-fare North Atlantic services. To meet a special Icelandic requirement the last of the series were CL-44Js, or Canadair 400s, with the fuselages lengthened by 15 ft and seating increased to 214. The Tynes used develop 5,730 hp.

France has produced one propeller-turbine transport which has been put into regular airline service, the Nord 262 high-wing monoplane with accommodation for 29 passengers. It is powered by two 1,065 hp Turbomeca Bastan VI engines, has a pressurised cabin, and entered service in 1964 with Air Inter on French domestic services. About one hundred have been acquired by airlines and other operators in Europe, the United States, Japan, Ceylon, North Africa and Madagascar.

The only large propeller-turbine powered passenger transport built in the United States was the Lockheed L-188 Electra which first flew on 6 December 1957. The Electra was similar to the Vickers Vanguard but smaller, and was a low-wing monoplane powered by four 3,750 hp Allison 501 propeller-turbines and had accommodation for up to 99 passengers.

The Electra was a superb aeroplane from the passengers' point of view and has given good service, but two fatal accidents caused by structural failure in flight, combined with the introduction of jets, kept orders down and only just over 170 were built. The type entered service with American Airlines and Eastern Air Lines in January 1959 and was also used in the United States by Braniff, National, Northwest, Pacific Southwest and Western Airlines. Electras were used in Europe by KLM

Aotearoa, a Tasman Empire Airways Lockheed L-188 Electra.

and did particularly well in Australasia and the Far East, fleets being used by Ansett-ANA, Qantas, and TAA in Australia, TEAL in New Zealand, Garuda Indonesian and Cathay Pacific. Some of American Airlines' Electras were sold to Varig in Brazil while others, together with two from Qantas, passed to Air California. More than ninety remained in service early in 1975.

One very interesting propeller-turbine transport is the NAMC YS-11 which was designed and built in Japan with the co-operation of Rolls-Royce which built special 3,060 hp Dart engines for it. The YS-11, produced in several versions, is a twin-engined low-wing monoplane with accommodation for up to sixty passengers. It first flew in August 1962 and entered airline service, in Japan, in April 1965. More than 180 YS-11s were constructed and Japan succeeded in exporting these aircraft to the United States, several South American countries, Canada and Europe. About seventy were supplied to Japanese airlines including All Nippon and Japan Domestic; Hawaiian Airlines leased three and the US carrier Piedmont Airlines bought 21; in South America, Argentine, Brazilian and Peruvian airlines bought them; Transair of Winnipeg has two; Korea and the Philippines bought them; and in Greece Olympic Airways acquired five with an option on five more. The YS-11 is the first Japanese transport ever sold outside Asia.

Apart from new aircraft designs employing propeller-turbines, some well-established piston-engined aircraft have been re-engined to achieve improved performance. All those in service are versions of the Convair-Liner described in Chapter 10. In Britain, Napier and Son fitted Eland propeller-turbines to a Convair CV-340 and a few of these were built or converted by Canadair as Convair or Canadair 540s. In the United States, 175 Convair-Liners were re-engined with 3,750 hp Allison 501s and designated CV-580 and a total of 68 CV-240s and CV-340s were fitted with 3,025 hp Rolls-Royce Darts after which they were known as CV-600s and CV-640s respectively. Most turbine-powered Convairs were used by US local service airlines.

	Span		Length		Passengers	Loaded weight	Cruising speed	Range
Vickers-Armstrongs Viscount V.701	93′	8½″	81′	10″	40/47	60,000 lb	324 mph	1,415 miles
Bristol Britannia 102	142′	3″	114′	0″	61/90	155,000 lb	362 mph	4,580 miles
Fokker F.27 Friendship	95′	1¾″	77′	1″	40/56	43,500 lb	295 mph	600 miles
Lockheed L-188 Electra	99′	0″	104′	8″	66/99	116,000 lb	405 mph	2,500 miles
Vickers-Armstrongs Vanguard	118′	0″	122′	10½″	126/139	141,000 lb	412 mph	2,070 miles
Handley Page Herald	94′	9″	75′	6″	56	43,000 lb	275 mph	700 miles
Avro 748	98′	6″	67′	0″	40/62	45,095 lb	287 mph	690 miles
Nord 262	71′	10½″	63′	3″	26/29	22,710 lb	230 mph	500 miles
NAMC YS-11	104′	11¾″	86′	3½″	46/60	54,010 lb	281 mph	680 miles
Canadair CL-44J	142′	3½″	151′	9¾″	214	210,000 lb	380 mph	5,260 miles

12

Jet Transports

On 2 May 1952 an event of great significance took place, for on that day a de Havilland Comet 1 jet transport of BOAC left London Airport for Johannesburg. That was the world's first passenger service to be flown by a turbojet-powered aeroplane, a vehicle destined to shrink the world to half its size by cutting journey times in two, and one which was to impose a changed outlook on distance with consequent enormous growth in world air traffic.

By today's standards the Comet was small, it carried only 36 passengers, for a jet it was comparatively slow, cruising at 490 mph, and its range was limited to 1,750 miles. But it revolutionised air transport, flying from London to Johannesburg in less than 24 hr. In August 1952 it began operating between London and Ceylon in $21\frac{1}{2}$ hr – a cut of more than 12 hr, and two months later Comets were flying to Singapore in 25 hr compared with $2\frac{1}{2}$ days by Argonaut. Then in April 1953 Comets cut the London–Tokyo time from 86 to $33\frac{1}{4}$ hr.

Air France and another French airline, UAT, both put Comets into operation, and a number of major airlines placed orders for this aeroplane which in performance was leading the world. Then in January 1954 a Comet disintegrated in flight near Elba and the type was grounded. After extensive examination and some modifications, Comets went back into service in March but just over a fortnight later another Comet broke up and all Comet 1s were withdrawn from passenger service. By that time more advanced Comet 2s were flying but all civil orders were cancelled and after modification these went to the Royal Air Force.

The initial Comets were each powered by four

The world's first jet airliner – the first prototype de Havilland Comet.

4,450 lb thrust de Havilland Ghost turbojets buried in the wing roots but subsequent Comets all had Rolls-Royce Avon turbojets of 10,500 lb thrust. In layout the Comets were low-wing monoplanes with sweptback leading edges but their tailplanes and fins were not swept back. The four-wheel bogie main undercarriage units retracted into the wings and there were twin nosewheels. The cabins were pressurised to give 8,000 ft interior conditions while the aircraft cruised at up to 40,000 ft.

After the failure of the Comet 1s there were no jet services until 1956 when the Soviet Tu-104 began operation; in the West it was not until October 1958 that jet services were resumed, by developed Comet 4s with BOAC and the first of the Boeing 707s with Pan American.

The new Comet 4 had a longer fuselage with seating for 60–81 passengers, was heavier and had improved performance. BOAC acquired nineteen Comet 4s, put them on most of the trunk routes and got more than ten years' work from them. The first North Atlantic jet services were operated in each direction on 4 October 1958, when BOAC introduced its Comet 4s.

From the Comet 4 was developed the Comet 4B with yet longer fuselage but shorter wing and the Comet 4C which combined Comet 4B fuselage with Comet 4 wing. These versions had accommodation for up to 101 passengers and the Comet 4B cruised at 530 mph. BEA began introduction of Comet 4Bs in 1959 and they have mostly been used by BEA and Olympic Airways. The Comet 4C's main operators were Middle East Airlines, United Arab Airlines, Sudan Airways, Kuwait Airways, Mexicana, and the Royal Air Force. Other Comet operators have included Aerolineas Argentinas, Air Ceylon, Dan-Air, Ecuatoriana, East African Airways and Malaysia-Singapore Airlines. A total of 112 Comets was built including 74 of the series 4 aircraft. Some are still in service.

Because they form a family of jet transports it is convenient to describe all the Boeing jetliners together although this story covers a period of over twenty years from the time in 1952 when the company began work on its first jet transport project. Known as the Boeing 707, but bearing the designation Model 367-80, the yellow and brown prototype made its first flight on 15 July 1954. It was a big-fuselage aeroplane with deep underfloor cargo and baggage holds and its wings had 35 degrees of sweepback. The main undercarriage comprised two inward-retracting four-wheel bogies. The outstanding feature was that the four turbojets were suspended in pods below and forward of the wing. This positioning of the engines allowed use of a much thinner high-speed wing with a large degree of elasticity.

The first production 707 was the Model 100 and it was this type which Pan American put into service over the North Atlantic in the autumn of 1958. It could carry up to 179 passengers, weighed 257,000 lb, was powered by four 12,500 lb thrust Pratt & Whitney JT3C engines and had a maximum-payload range of less than 3,000 miles. It cruised at 570 mph and had to make an intermediate stop on westbound Atlantic flights.

The Boeing 707-100 series was not intended for North Atlantic operation and was replaced on this route by the 707-300 Intercontinental which appeared in 1959. This later version was more than 8 ft longer and had 15 ft greater span. Its take-off weight at 312,000 lb was 55,000 lb greater and its range was increased to 4,630 miles. Seating was increased to provide for up to 189 passengers. The main versions of the Intercontinental were the -320 series with Pratt & Whitney JT4 turbojets and the -420 with Rolls-Royce Conway bypass engines. Two special versions of the early 707s were the short-fuselage -138, built for Qantas, and the -227 higher-powered model for Braniff, which needed better take-off performance at some of its more difficult airports.

Final development of the 707 came with the introduction of Pratt & Whitney JT3D turbofans of 18,000 lb thrust. These engines gave better take-off performance and, combined with some modifications to the aircraft including a further increase of 3 ft 4 in in span, increased the range to 6,160 miles. The two main versions are the 707-300B passenger aircraft and the -300C with large cargo door. Some of the earlier aircraft, including the Qantas aeroplanes, were brought to B standard.

A direct development of the Boeing 707 was the 165-passenger Model 720 which was produced with JT3C engines and, as the B model, with JT3D turbofans. The 720B could cruise at up to 622 mph.

Boeing 707-320B and C aircraft are still in production and over 900 civil 707s and 720s have been built as well as 820 military transport and tanker versions.

Having produced the 707 and 720 for the medium- and long-distance routes, Boeing decided to build a short- to medium-range aircraft for routes over which the 720 would be uneconomic. This resulted in the Model 727 with three rear-mounted engines and T-tail. The fuselage cross-section of the 727 remained the same as that of the 707/720 but the aircraft had a new wing with highly developed flaps and slats to allow operation from short runways. The Boeing 727 entered service in February 1964 with Eastern Air Lines and United Air Lines and soon attracted orders from all over the world. In basic layout it could carry 28 passengers in four-across first class seats and 66 tourist class passengers in six-across seating but an all-tourist version could carry 131 passengers.

From the basic 727-100, Boeing developed the Model 200 with an increase in fuselage length of 20 ft and with seating for up to 189 passengers. The 727 is one of the most successful short/medium-

One of the most successful jetliners is the Boeing 727, seen here in Alaska Airlines' livery.

haul transports ever and by the end of December 1974 a total of 1,195 had been ordered, and the 1,088 delivered had carried more than 660 mn passengers. By the same date Boeing jet airliners of all types had flown nearly 22,000 mn miles in airline service.

In 1965 Boeing began production of a smaller, twin-jet aircraft. This was the Model 737 which employed the same fuselage cross-section but had its 14,000 lb thrust JT8D engines mounted close beneath the wing. It has a low position tailplane, tall fin and rudder and twin-wheel main under-carriage units. Maximum seating in the original -100 model is for 103/115. Lufthansa and United Air Lines placed the first orders and the type entered service in the spring of 1968. A development, the 737-200, can carry as many as 125 passengers. QC (Quick Change) models exist of the 727 and 737 and can be converted in a very short time so that they can carry passengers by day and cargo at night. More than 420 Boeing 737s have been ordered.

Following production of its smallest jet transport, Boeing began design and production of the biggest aeroplane ever to go into passenger service. This is the Boeing 747 which can carry over 500 passengers although most are initially being equipped to carry about 360 passengers. In appearance the 747 resembles a scaled-up 707 but is a truly massive aeroplane, with the flight deck and first class lounge and bar on a separate deck above the main passenger cabins. The 747 has 50 ft greater span than the 707, is more than 78 ft longer, has more than twice the power and is well over double the weight.

The cabins of the 747 are 20 ft wide and the seating is arranged in three blocks with two aisles dividing the cabins lengthwise. The floor is more than 16 ft above the ground and the height to the top of the fin when the aircraft is at rest is more than 63 ft.

The thrust of each of the four Pratt & Whitney JT9D turbofans is 47,000 lb and the engine intakes have a diameter of 8 ft. The main undercarriage has sixteen wheels comprising four sets of four-wheel bogies. A cargo version with swing-nose can carry more than 100 tons.

Pan American operated the first 747 service, from New York to London, in January 1970, and more than 280 have been ordered by nearly forty airlines including Air Canada, Air France, Air-India, Alitalia, American Airlines, BOAC, Japan Air Lines, KLM, Lufthansa, Qantas, SAS, South African Airways, Swissair, TWA and United Air Lines.

The second big jet to appear was the Douglas DC-8 which first flew on 30 May 1958. In layout the DC-8 very closely followed the Boeing 707 but had less sharply sweptback wings and a rather more finely swept fin and rudder. The first DC-8s, the -10 model, entered service on 18 September 1959 with Delta Air Lines and United Air Lines. They were powered by four 13,500 lb thrust Pratt & Whitney JT3C turbojets and had accommodation for up to 179 passengers. Then followed four more versions: the -20 with 15,800 lb thrust engines, the -30 long-range version with Pratt & Whitney engines, the -40 long-range version with Rolls-Royce Conway bypass engines, and the -50 which was similar to the -30 but with Pratt & Whitney turbofans. A development of the -50 was the DC-8F Jet Trader with large cargo door.

In August 1961 a DC-8 became the first jet transport aircraft to exceed the speed of sound, when it reached 667 mph (Mach 1·012) in a shallow dive. The speed of sound is referred to as Mach 1 and is about 660 mph at high altitude but it varies with temperature.

Early in 1966 the first of a new series of DC-8s appeared under the title Series 60. The first of these

was the DC-8-61 which retained the DC-8-50 wing but had its fuselage lengthened by 37 ft to provide accommodation for up to 259 passengers. This type entered service in February 1967. Next came the long-range DC-8-62 with 6 ft increase in span but only just under 7 ft extra fuselage length – it had seating for up to 189 passengers and entered service with SAS in May 1967. The DC-8-63 combined the very long fuselage of the DC-8-61 with the wing of the DC-8-62 and entered service in July 1967 with KLM. All versions of the DC-8-60, including the all-cargo and passenger/cargo versions, are powered by four 18,000 lb thrust Pratt & Whitney JT3D turbofans. A total of 556 DC-8s of all versions was built, with the last delivered in 1972.

To meet short-haul requirements Douglas built the DC-9 which first flew in February 1965. This is a low-wing monoplane with two rear-mounted engines, T-tail and four-wheel main undercarriage. To ensure good handling characteristics at low speed the wings have only 24 degrees of sweepback. Like the DC-8, the DC-9 has been produced in a number of versions. The first type was the DC-9-10 with 12,250 lb or 14,000 lb thrust Pratt & Whitney JT8D turbofans and seats for up to ninety passengers, and it entered service on 8 December 1965, with Delta Air Lines.

The second version of the DC-9 was the -30 with 4 ft increase in span, 15 ft increase in length and accommodation for up to 115 passengers. The DC-9-30 went into service on 1 February 1967 with Eastern Air Lines and this is the version which has been ordered in the greatest numbers.

Two other versions were designed specifically for SAS. The first was the -40 with 14,500 lb thrust engines and yet another 6 ft added to the fuselage to increase passenger accommodation to 125, entering service in March 1968. In January 1969 SAS began operating the DC-9-20, a ninety-passenger aircraft with improved aerodrome performance and combining the -10 fuselage with -30 wings. The only -20s were the ten supplied to SAS.

The 133-ft long 139-passenger DC-9-50 made its first flight on 17 December 1974. DC-9s are still in production and more than 820 have been sold to airlines in the Americas, Europe, Australia, Japan, Saudi Arabia and South Korea.

In addition to the Boeing and Douglas series of jetliners there were two other US four-engined designs which entered service, the Convair CV-880 and CV-990 Coronado.

The Convairs were short/medium-range aeroplanes of high performance. They were of similar layout to the Boeing 707 and Douglas DC-8 but had narrower bodies, with five-across tourist seating, and were faster. The General Electric CJ-805

◀ This view shows the enormous size of the Boeing 747.

One of the long-bodied Douglas DC-8-60 aircraft. This example is a DC-8-61 of Eastern Air Lines.

powered CV-880 was designed to meet a TWA requirement but first entered service with Delta Air Lines, in May 1960. Maximum accommodation was for 109 in coach class or 130 in high-density seating. Only 65 CV-880s were built and they were mainly used by Delta, CAT in Formosa, Cathay Pacific Airways, Japan Air Lines, Northeast Airlines, TWA and VIASA of Venezuela.

To meet an American Airlines requirement for a US transcontinental aeroplane the larger CV-990 Coronado was produced. This type had 16,000 lb thrust General Electric turbofans and could carry up to 121 tourist class passengers or 158 in high-density seating. Increased speed was obtained by the addition of four shock bodies which looked like inverted canoes and extended behind the wing. These were used to carry extra fuel. The Convairs were popular with passengers and, although regarded as rather 'hot' aeroplanes, they built up an extremely good safety record. Delays during the development programme of the CV-990 cut into its sales chances and only 37 were built. CV-990s

Sven Viking, one of SAS's fleet of Sud-Aviation Caravelle IIIs.

entered service with American Airlines and Swissair in March 1962, other operators of the type being Alaska Airlines, APSA of Peru, Garuda Indonesian Airways, Lebanese International (LIA), Middle East Airlines, SAS, Spantax of Spain, and Varig of Brazil.

The most successful European jet transport is undoubtedly the French Sud-Aviation Caravelle which was the first jet airliner to have rear-mounted engines. The Caravelle is an extremely beautiful twin-engined low-wing monoplane with clean 20

degree sweptback wing and mid-mounted tailplane. The Caravelle first flew in May 1955 and the Series I aircraft entered service in May 1959 with Air France on the Paris–Rome–Istanbul route and with SAS between Copenhagen and Cairo.

The original Caravelles were powered by two 10,500 lb thrust Rolls-Royce Avon turbojets, and most have been built with accommodation for eighty passengers. The type has undergone continuous development, being fitted with more powerful engines and refined in various ways, the biggest changes being in the 89/109-passenger Super B model with lengthened fuselage and 14,000 lb thrust Pratt & Whitney JT8D turbofans. The Caravelle Super B was introduced by Finnair on its Helsinki – Milan service in August 1964. The Caravelle 11R with large cargo door is just over 2 ft longer than the Super B and the 128-passenger Caravelle 12B is nearly 119 ft long.

Caravelles saw widescale service in Europe, the Americas, North Africa, the Near and Middle East, and when it was ordered by United Air Lines it became the first French airliner to operate in the United States. A total of 280 was built and many are equipped for automatic landing.

As a successor to the Comet, de Havilland (now absorbed by Hawker Siddeley) designed the D.H.121 Trident for BEA. The Trident closely resembles the Boeing 727 but it flew a year earlier than the Boeing and was the first of the three-engined jet transports. The 9,850 lb thrust Rolls-Royce Spey engines were mounted one inside the rear fuselage and one each side. BEA ordered 24 Trident 1s and began operating them as 96-passenger aircraft in the spring of 1964. In June 1965 a Trident made the first automatic landing by an aircraft operating a passenger service and all BEA Tridents have autoland capability.

An improved Trident, the 1E, with increased power and leading edge slats to improve take-off

and landing, first flew at the end of 1964, and in 1968 BEA began operating the longer-range 89/97-passenger Trident 2E with three 11,930 lb thrust Spey turbofans. The latest version is the Trident 3B which made its first flight in December 1969. This type, 26 of which were ordered by BEA, is 16 ft 5 in longer, can accommodate up to 171 passengers, and has a 5,250 lb thrust Rolls-Royce RB.162 booster engine in the tail in addition to its three 11,930 lb thrust Speys. In spite of its increased size and weight, the Trident 3B has better take-off performance than the Trident 2E but its cruising speed is lower. A total of 117 Tridents has been ordered. In addition to those operated by BEA, Tridents have been sold to Air Ceylon, British Air Services (BKS), CAAC (China), Channel Airways, Cyprus Airways, Iraqi Airways, Kuwait Airways and Pakistan International Airlines.

The largest British jet transports are the Vickers VC10 and Super VC10 which were designed for BOAC. These are low-wing monoplanes with $32\frac{1}{2}$ degrees sweepback, four rear-mounted engines and large high-mounted tailplane. These two types are essentially the same except that the Super VC10 is 13 ft longer, 23,000 lb heavier, has slightly more power, and has a fuel tank in the fin to give increased range. Maximum accommodation is for 151 in the standard VC10 and 174 in the Super VC10. Both

One of BOAC's fleet of Vickers-Armstrongs Super VC10s. The air-brakes can be seen in the extended position above the wings.

types have a pair of Rolls-Royce Conway bypass engines mounted on each side of the rear fuselage and these each develop 21,000/22,500 lb of thrust. Some VC10s have a large cargo door in the port side of the forward fuselage. The VC10s have outstanding take-off performance, land relatively slowly and are well liked by both crews and passengers. Unfortunately the type appeared too late to attract worthwhile orders, because the world's airlines were already equipped with big jets, and only 54 were built, including fourteen for the Royal Air Force. BOAC introduced VC10s on the London–Lagos route in April 1964 and Super VC10s began working the London–New York route a year later. British United Airways, Ghana Airways, MEA and Nigeria Airways have all operated VC10s, and East African Airways has a fleet of Super VC10s.

The most successful British jet transport is the BAC One-Eleven. The British Aircraft Corporation is the successor to Vickers-Armstrongs and Bristol Aircraft, and all the experience gained with the Viscount, Vanguard, VC10 and Britannia went into the design of the One-Eleven which is a twin-jet short-haul aeroplane intended as a successor to the Viscount and Convair-Liner category of aircraft. In layout the BAC One-Eleven is a low-wing monoplane with 20 degree sweepback, two rear-mounted Rolls-Royce Spey turbofans, and T-tail. The main versions are the series 200, 400 and 500.

The series 200, with 10,330 lb thrust engines and accommodation for up to 89 passengers, entered service with British United Airways and Braniff in April 1965. The series 400 was generally similar but modified to meet the requirements of United States operators, thirty being ordered by American Airlines. The series 500 is nearly 14 ft longer, has a 5 ft increase in span, 12,550 lb thrust engines and accommodation for up to 109 passengers. This larger version entered service with BEA in November 1968. Latest version is the One-Eleven 475 for use from

short runways. First flown in 1970, it was ordered by Air Malawi, Air Pacific (Fiji) and Faucett (Peru).

More than 200 BAC One-Elevens have been ordered, with more than a third going to operators in the Americas.

Just as BAC produced a jet successor to the Viscount so Fokker built a jet successor to the F.27 Friendship. The Dutch aircraft is the 55/79-passenger F.28 Fellowship which has two rear-mounted 9,850 lb thrust Rolls-Royce Spey Junior turbofans. In order to provide good aerodrome performance, the low-mounted wing has only 16 degrees of sweepback and the F.28 has already proved its ability to operate from unpaved dirt runways. Unlike all other jet transports the F.28 has petal-type air-brakes formed by the fuselage tail cone. The Dutch jet first flew on 9 May 1967, and entered service on 28 March 1969 with Braathens S.A.F.E. in Norway. By the end of January 1975 a total of 92 F.28s had been ordered and Itavia, Martinair Holland, Mac. Robertson Miller Airlines, Ghana Airways, Nigeria Airways and Iberia are among the 30 operators in 23 countries.

In concluding the story of the jet transport two other types deserve mention, one of which might easily have been the first jet airliner to fly and the other which was never completed.

Avro Canada, in 1946, began design of the C-102

Jetliner which was a low-wing fifty-passenger monoplane with four 3,600 lb thrust Rolls-Royce Derwent turbojets. Only one example was completed and it made its first flight on 10 August 1949, exactly two weeks after the first Comet. It made a mail flight from Toronto to New York in April 1950 and is reported to have, on at least one occasion, exceeded 500 mph in level flight.

The uncompleted jet transport was the Vickers Type 1000 which was cancelled in 1955 after reaching an advanced stage of construction. It was designed for the Royal Air Force and BOAC and would have been a low-wing monoplane with four Rolls-Royce Conway engines buried in the wing. The V.1000 was to have been capable of North Atlantic operation, would have had six-abreast seating, and weighed about 225,000 lb loaded.

Soviet jet transports are described in Chapter 14.

	Span		Length		Passengers	Loaded weight	Cruising speed	Range
de Havilland Comet 1	115′	0″	93′	0″	36	105,000 lb	490 mph	1,750 miles
de Havilland Comet 4	115′	0″	111′	6″	60/81	162,000 lb	516 mph	3,225 miles
Sud Caravelle I	112′	6¼″	105′	0″	80	95,901 lb	460 mph	1,035 miles
Boeing 707-320B	145′	9″	152′	11″	189	327,000 lb	550 mph	6,160 miles
Convair CV-990	120′	0″	139′	2½″	106	253,000 lb	625 mph	3,920 miles
de Havilland Trident 1	89′	10″	114′	9″	77/103	115,000 lb	576 mph	1,485 miles
Boeing 727-100	108′	0″	133′	2″	94/131	142,000 lb	570 mph	2,050 miles
Vickers Super VC10	146′	2″	171′	8″	139	335,000 lb	550 mph	4,720 miles
BAC One-Eleven 200	88′	6″	93′	6″	79	78,500 lb	507 mph	960 miles
Douglas DC-8-63	148′	5″	187′	5″	259	350,000 lb	600 mph	4,500 miles
Douglas DC-9-30	93′	5″	119′	3½″	105/115	98,000 lb	565 mph	1,725 miles
Boeing 737-100	93′	0″	94′	0″	103/115	104,000 lb	570 mph	1,840 miles
Fokker F.28	77′	4¼″	89′	10¾″	55/65	62,000 lb	519 mph	1,162 miles
Boeing 747-200B	195′	8″	231′	4″	500	775,000 lb	625 mph	5,790 miles

13

Feederliners

An important class of transport aircraft, which can be only briefly mentioned here, is the small feederliner used on short-stage routes with low-density traffic. In the 1930s Britain played a leading part in producing this type of aircraft and the most important were the de Havilland D.H.84 Dragon, D.H.86 Express and D.H.89 Dragon Rapide.

The de Havilland company, in 1932, produced the D.H.83 Fox Moth single-engined biplane which, on the power of a single 130 hp de Havilland Gipsy Major engine, could carry a pilot and four passengers. The British factory built 98, two were built in Australia and, as late as 1946 de Havilland Canada embarked on production of 54. The Fox Moth was adopted by a number of airlines in the United Kingdom, Australia, Canada, India, New Zealand and elsewhere, and it proved very success-

ful; but there was a need for a larger aeroplane.

At about the same time, in 1932, the Iraqi Air Force and Edward Hillman, a bus operator in southeast England, had need of a twin-engined aeroplane with double the capacity of the Fox Moth. The result was the D.H.84 Dragon which first flew in November 1932. It was a simple wood and fabric biplane powered by two 130 hp Gipsy Major engines and had accommodation for pilot and six passengers. The Dragon could operate from small fields, and it became popular with pioneer airlines in Britain and many parts of the world. It was used by Highland Airways to develop services from Inverness to Orkney and Shetland, by Hillman's Airways for cheap fare cross-Channel services, by Jersey Airways for the first sustained services between Jersey and the mainland, and by almost all the operators of

City of Cardiff was one of the de Havilland 84 Dragons used by Railway Air Services on United Kingdom domestic services.

British internal air services. Dragons were used by a number of air forces and private owners and by airlines in Australia, Brazil, Egypt, India, Kenya and New Zealand. It was a Dragon which inaugurated Aer Lingus services from Dublin. In Britain de Havilland built 115 Dragons and in 1942–43 another 87 were built in Australia.

The next de Havilland transport, the D.H.86, was built to meet an Australian requirement for an aircraft capable of operating the Brisbane–

Singapore section of the Australia–England route when the service was opened in December 1934. The D.H.86 was another wood and fabric biplane, though of much cleaner appearance than the Dragon, and fitted with four 200 hp Gipsy Six engines. It could carry two crew and ten to twelve passengers. Qantas Empire Airways operated five, and Imperial Airways had a total of twelve which were used on European services, between Khartoum and West Africa and in the Far East. Railway Air Services used D.H.86s on the London–Belfast–Glasgow Royal Mail route, and Jersey Airways had eight. They were also used by other British airlines, by Aer Lingus, DHY in Turkey, Misr in Egypt, Union Airways in New Zealand, Tata in India, Pluna in Uruguay, and a number of other Australian airlines. Sixty-two D.H.86s were built.

Also first built in 1934 was the D.H.89 Dragon Rapide, known for a time as the Dragon Six. This incorporated features of the Dragon and D.H.86 and was a five/eight-passenger biplane with two 200 hp Gipsy Six engines. In layout it was similar to the Dragon but had finely tapered wings and trousered undercarriage as well as the greater power. The Rapide, as it was generally known, remained in production until 1946 and about 700 were built. These aircraft played an important part in developing air transport in most parts of the world, they were

operated with wheel, float and ski undercarriages and were used in large numbers by airlines throughout the British Commonwealth and in many other countries.

There were numerous other types of small feederliner in service before the 1939–45 war, such as the Airspeed Ferry, Courier and Envoy, the Westland Wessex, the Spartan Cruiser, the twin-engined Monospars, the Farman F.430, Caudron Goëland, Breda 44 and Caproni Bergamaschi Borea, but the de Havilland types were by far the most used and the most important.

When the war ended de Havillands were quick to design a modern feederliner, the D.H.104 Dove. This was an all-metal low-wing monoplane with retractable nosewheel undercarriage, two 340 hp Gipsy Queen engines and accommodation for two crew and five to eleven passengers. The Dove first flew on 25 September 1945, and more than 540 were built including the military Devons. Doves were used by airlines in many parts of the world and a large number were sold in the United States.

In 1950 the larger D.H.114 Heron appeared. This was capable of carrying up to seventeen passengers, had four 250 hp Gipsy Queen engines and was produced in two main versions, one with retractable and the other with non-retractable undercarriage. Nearly 150 Herons were built and many went into airline service throughout the world.

The four-engined Miles Marathon, which first flew in May 1946, saw limited airline service as did the twin-engined Percival Prince and the short take-off Scottish Aviation Twin Pioneer.

A whole family of successful feederliners was produced in Toronto by de Havilland Canada. The first was the single-engined Beaver strut-braced high-wing monoplane with 450 hp Pratt & Whitney Wasp Junior engine and seats for pilot and six passengers. More than 1,600 Beavers were built following the appearance of the prototype in August 1947 and many have been used to serve remote rugged regions where few other aircraft could operate. Beavers can be fitted with wheels, floats or skis, and the latest version of the aircraft is propeller-turbine powered. In 1951 an enlarged development appeared as the ten/fourteen-passenger Otter which had a 600 hp Pratt & Whitney Wasp engine. A total of 466 Otters was built and some saw airline service, the landplane and amphibian versions operating Qantas services to remote parts of New Guinea and Papua, and float seaplanes working services in northern Norway.

The latest de Havilland Canada type to go into service is the STOL (short take-off and landing) Twin Otter of which over 450 have been ordered. This type is a high-wing semi-cantilever monoplane powered by two 579/652 hp Pratt & Whitney PT6A propeller-turbines and capable of carrying two crew and up to twenty passengers. Most are fitted with non-retractable nosewheel undercarriages but twin floats or combined wheel/ski undercarriages can be used. With full load the Twin Otter can take-off with a run of only 820 ft. It is in service with airlines in many parts of the world including the commuter or third-level airlines in the United States.

In Australia, de Havilland designed and built a three-engined feederliner which first flew in January 1948. This was the eight-passenger Drover, a low-wing monoplane with tailwheel undercarriage and 145 hp Gipsy Major engines. Only a small batch was built and these saw service with Qantas, Trans-Australia Airlines, the Royal Flying Doctor Service and Fiji Airways. Some of the ambulance Drovers were re-engined with 180 hp Lycomings.

Switzerland has produced a successful feederliner in the Pilatus Porter and Turbo-Porter single-engined high-wing monoplanes but few have been operated by airlines. Germany, too, builds small feederliners, the single-engined Dornier Do 27, and the twin-engined Do 28 and Do 28D Skyservant. These are all high-wing cantilever monoplanes, and the Skyservant, which is the latest, has seats for up to thirteen passengers and is powered by two 380 hp Lycoming engines. With full load it can take off and reach a height of 50 ft in a distance of only 1,140 ft and with power on and flaps down it can fly at speeds as low as 40 mph.

A modern British aeroplane which is proving as successful as the Dragon Rapide is the Britten-Norman Islander which is built in the Isle of Wight, Belgium and Rumania. This is a short take-off cantilever high-wing monoplane powered by two 260 hp Lycoming engines and capable of carrying ten people and of operating from short rough landing fields. Its take-off run can be as short as 520 ft. The Islander first flew in June 1965, well over 600 have been ordered and several hundred were in airline service by the beginning of 1975. A three-engined Islander, the Trislander, with the third engine mounted on the tail, went into production in 1971.

Over the last few years there has been an enormous development of what are known as commuter or third-level airline services in the United States, with a smaller growth of such operations in Australia and elsewhere. A wide range of small aeroplanes is being used on these services including Doves, Herons, Twin Otters, Islanders and Skyservants. Beech Aircraft Corporation in Kansas has produced a miniature airliner largely to serve such airlines, the Beech 99 twin-engined low-wing monoplane powered by 550 hp Pratt & Whitney PT6A propeller-turbines and having accommodation for two crew and fifteen passengers.

	Span	Length	Passengers	Loaded weight	Cruising speed	Range
de Havilland Dragon	47′ 4″	34′ 6″	6	4,500 lb	109–114 mph	545 miles
de Havilland 86	64′ 6″	46′ 1″	10/12	10,000 lb	145 mph	760 miles
de Havilland Dragon Rapide	48′ 0″	34′ 6″	5/8	5,500 lb	132 mph	580 miles
de Havilland Dove	57′ 0″	39′ 4″	5/11	8,500 lb	165–179 mph	1,000 miles
de Havilland Heron 1	71′ 6″	48′ 6″	17	13,000 lb	160 mph	805 miles
DHC.2 Beaver	48′ 0″	30′ 3″	6	4,820 lb	137 mph	455 miles
DHC.6 Twin Otter	65′ 0″	51′ 9″	19/20	12,500 lb	190–202 mph	760 miles
Britten-Norman Islander	49′ 0″	35′ 8″	9	6,000 lb	155 mph	810 miles
Beechcraft 99	45′ 10½″	44′ 6¾″	15	10,400 lb	252 mph	375 miles

14

Soviet Airliners

The first regular air services in which there was Soviet participation were those between Königsberg and Moscow which started in May 1922, and on these Fokker aircraft were used. German Junkers-F 13s and Dornier Komets flew some early Soviet domestic services.

The Soviet-designed U-2 single-engined light biplanes (later known as Po-2s) and a number of versions of the R-5 biplane saw service on Soviet air routes, as did such single-engined monoplanes as the AK 1, Kalinin K4 and K5 and Stal-2 and 3, while some remote areas were served by single-engined Sh-2 amphibian flying-boats. However, in April 1929 the Soviet Union's first three-engined airliner was completed. This was the ANT-9, a high-wing monoplane with corrugated metal skin. It had accommodation for two crew and nine

passengers, was used on Deruluft's Moscow–Berlin service and operated on both wheel and ski undercarriages. A twin-engined version was also produced, and a total of about seventy built.

In May 1934 the ANT-20 *Maxim Gorki* eight-engined monoplane made its first flight but was lost in an inflight collision and never went into service. Developed from the *Maxim Gorki* was the six-engined ANT-20bis (also known as the PS-124) which could carry up to 64 passengers. It is believed to have been completed in 1939, and was reported to have gone into service in May 1940 between Moscow and Mineral'nyye Vody, but only one is known to have been built.

The most advanced pre-war Soviet transport aircraft was the ANT-35 (PS-35), a smooth-skinned low-wing monoplane powered by two 850 hp M-85 radial engines. It had a retractable undercarriage, seats for ten passengers, and a cruising speed of 223 mph. Only small-scale production was undertaken but the type did go into service in July 1937 with Aeroflot on the Moscow–Riga–Stockholm route.

The Soviet Union, not having been very successful with home-designed transport aircraft, bought a small number of American Douglas DC-3s and these worked alongside the ANT-35s. DC-3s were then built in the USSR under licence as PS-84s and entered service on Aeroflot routes in 1940. In 1942 they were redesignated Lisunov Li-2s and throughout the war years and for some time after formed the backbone of the Soviet civil air fleets.

The first Soviet transport aeroplane to go into large-scale production was the Ilyushin Il-12 which made its first flight early in 1946 and entered service with Aeroflot in 1947. This was a straightforward all-metal low-wing monoplane with retractable nose-wheel undercarriage, powered by two 1,650/1,755 hp Shvetsov ASh-82FN radial engines, and originally had accommodation for 27 passengers on domestic and 21 passengers on international routes. Some Il-12s were operated as freighters and had double loading doors on the port side.

Large numbers of Il-12s were operated by Aeroflot, and on the transcontinental route from Moscow to Vladivostok they completed the journey in 33 hr with nine intermediate stops.

ČSA of Czechoslovakia operated Il-12s, with 28–32 seats, and others were used by Polskie Linie Lotnicze 'LOT', the Chinese airline CAAC, and by the Soviet Air Force. The number of Il-12s constructed is not known but a figure as high as 3,000 has been reported.

A development of the Il-12 was the Il-14 which first flew in 1953. This was generally similar but had 1,630/1,900 hp ASh-82T engines, a modified wing with squarer tips, and a new vertical fin and rudder. It also incorporated a number of aerodynamic improvements, including cleaner engine nacelles. The new aircraft is believed to have first entered service with the Soviet Air Force and then, in 1954, the civil Il-14P was introduced by Aeroflot, with seating for eighteen passengers. In 1956 the 28/32-passenger Il-14M version appeared. Cargo versions were the Il-14G and Il-14T.

Very large numbers of Il-14s went to Aeroflot and others were used by Air Guinée, Air Mali, CAAC, ČSA, Cubana, Deutsche Lufthansa (DDR) (later Interflug), JAT in Yugoslavia, Malév, Polskie Linie Lotnicze, Tabso, Tarom, Ukamps in North Korea, Yemen Airlines and United Arab Airlines. They were also used by a number of air forces and heads of State.

An Aeroflot Tupolev Tu-104A on its landing approach with wheels and flaps lowered.

Il-14s were also built in East Germany as VEB Il-14s, and a number of versions were built in Czechoslovakia as the Avia-14 series. It has been reported that 3,500 Il-14s were built and many are still in service with Aeroflot, some other airlines and air forces.

There was nothing outstanding about the Il-12 and Il-14 but they were useful aircraft and did a good job for Aeroflot in developing its massive network of routes.

The Soviet Union made two attempts at pro-

ducing larger four-engined piston transports, the Il-18 and Tupolev Tu-70, both completed in 1947, but neither type went into production.

In 1953 a major programme was begun to produce more modern aircraft for Aeroflot and led to design and construction of a number of types of turbojet and propeller-turbine powered aircraft, the first of these being the Tupolev Tu-104 twin-jet based on the Tu-16 bomber.

The Tu-104 made its first flight on 17 June 1955, and on 15 September 1956 entered regular service on the Moscow–Omsk–Irkutsk route. This Soviet aircraft was the second type of jet transport to go into commercial service and the first to remain in continuous service – between September 1956 and the autumn of 1958 it was the only jet transport in airline service anywhere.

In layout the Tu-104 is a low-wing monoplane with sweptback wing and tail surfaces and two engines buried in the wing roots. The main units of the undercarriage, each with a four-wheel bogie, retract backwards into streamlined fairings which protrude behind the wing trailing edge, a practice followed in later Tupolev designs.

Tu-104s drastically cut journey times over the great distances in the USSR but were uneconomic with accommodation for only fifty passengers; so, in 1957, a modified version, the Tu-104A, appeared with seating for seventy. This was followed by the 100-seat Tu-104B in 1958. It is believed that some Tu-104As were modified to become 85/100-seat Tu-104Ds and that in 1967 some Tu-104Bs were re-arranged to carry up to 115 passengers.

The original Tu-104 had two 14,881 lb thrust Mikulin RD-3 or AM-3 turbojets but the Tu-104A had 19,180 lb thrust AM-3M and the Tu-104B 21,384 lb thrust RD-3M-500 engines.

Tu-104s were introduced on many of Aeroflot's domestic and international routes, six were sup-plied to ČSA, and some Soviet Air Force examples were used for astronaut training. It appears that about 200 Tu-104 series aircraft were built and many are still in service.

As far as is known the Tu-104 was the first civil airliner to be fitted with tail parachutes for emergency braking after landing.

In 1959 two large new propeller-turbine powered Soviet transports entered service, the Antonov An-10 and the Ilyushin Il-18. The Il-18 was a new design, having no connection with the piston-engined Il-18 of 1947. The new aircraft was a clean low-wing monoplane of all-metal construction with fully retractable nosewheel undercarriage and production aircraft were each powered by four 4,000 hp Ivchenko AI-20 turbines driving four-blade propellers.

The prototype Il-18 flew on 4 July 1957, and after a period of trials and cargo operation the type entered service with Aeroflot on 20 April 1959 on the Moscow–Alma Ata and Moscow–Adler/Sochi routes. It was put into large-scale production, well over 500 have been built, and by 1967 they were carrying forty per cent of all Aeroflot's traffic. Apart from forming the backbone of the Soviet civil air fleets, the Il-18 proved to be the most successful Soviet transport in terms of export orders and was adopted by Air Guinée, Air Mali, CAAC,

One of ČSA's red and white long-range Ilyushin Il-18Ds.

ČSA, Cubana, Deutsche Lufthansa of East Germany, Ghana Airways, Malév, Polskie Linie Lotnicze, Tabso (now Balkan), Tarom, United Arab Airlines and, more recently, Air Mauritanie. Il-18s are also used by several air forces.

The first Il-18s had accommodation for eighty passengers but the type was steadily developed to have improved performance and increased capacity, and the Il-18D and Il-18E versions can carry up to 122 passengers in summer when less space is required for stowage of passengers' heavy clothing. After

over fifteen years' service very large numbers of Il-18s are still in operation.

The An-10 was a very different aeroplane. Like the Il-18 it had a circular-section pressurised fuselage and four 4,000 hp AI-20 propeller-turbines, but it was designed for carriage of heavy traffic in areas where aerodrome standards were poor and it had to be able to operate from unpaved surfaces. It was a high-wing monoplane and the undercarriage retracted into bulges low down on the sides of the fuselage.

When it went into service with Aeroflot on 22 July 1959 on the Moscow–Simferopol route, the An-10 had accommodation for 85 passengers but the improved An-10A could carry a hundred passengers. Quite large numbers of An-10 and An-10A aircraft were built and from the type was developed the An-12 civil and military transport with rear under-fuselage loading doors. An-12s operate Aeroflot cargo services over the entire length of the Soviet Union. Ghana Airways and Cubana each had an An-12 and Polskie Linie Lotnicze and Bulair of Bulgaria each operated at least two. Aeroflot has used An-12s in the Arctic and Antarctic and some of these have heated brake-equipped skis. The Indian, Indonesian, Iraqi and United Arab Republic air forces have all operated An-12s.

In 1961 Aeroflot introduced the biggest and fastest propeller-turbine aeroplane ever to go into passenger service, the Tupolev Tu-114 which had four 12,000 hp Kuznetsov NK-12M propeller-turbines, a span of 167 ft 7¾ in, a loaded weight of 385,809 lb, could carry up to 220 passengers and cruise at 478·46 mph with a top speed of no less than 540 mph. Its maximum range was 5,396 nautical miles.

Although the Tu-114 could carry 220 passengers, it was normally equipped to carry 120–145 passengers in a number of separate cabins and it had a kitchen on the lower deck. It went into regular operation on 24 April 1961 over the Moscow–Khabarovsk route, a distance of 3,723 nautical miles which it covered in 8¼ hr. On 7 January 1963 the Tu-114 opened Aeroflot's first transatlantic service when it began flying between Moscow and Havana with a refuelling stop at Murmansk, and on 4 November 1966 Tu-114s began a nonstop Moscow–Montreal service. These aircraft were also used on the Moscow–Delhi and Moscow–Accra routes and, from April 1967, on a joint Aeroflot/Japan Air Lines service between Tokyo and Moscow. About thirty Tu-114s are thought to have been built.

Having produced jet and propeller-turbine powered airliners for the heavy-traffic and long-distance routes, the Soviet Union undertook the design and construction of turbine-powered aeroplanes for use on the short-stage and feeder routes, and in October 1962 two new aircraft in this category were introduced. These were the high-wing propeller-turbine Antonov An-24 and the twin-jet low-wing Tupolev Tu-124.

The An-24 is a twin-engined aeroplane of similar size and layout to the well-known Fokker Friendship. It exists in several versions carrying 37 to 50 passengers or cargo and is in service in large numbers in the USSR and in small numbers in China, East

Germany, Bulgaria, Cuba, Guinée, Mali, Mongolia, Poland, Rumania and the Egyptian Arab Republic. The engines are two 2,100/2,800 hp Ivchenko AI-24 propeller-turbines, and one version of the An-24, the An-24RV, has an auxiliary turbojet in the rear of the starboard engine nacelle. This allows maximum loads to be carried from aerodromes at elevations up to 8,200 ft and in temperatures as high as 45 degrees C and also assists in the event of a main engine failure.

The Tu-124 is virtually a three-quarter scale Tu-104. It is powered by two 11,905 lb thrust Soloviev D-20P turbofans, carries 44–56 passengers and can operate from unpaved aerodromes. Aeroflot has about a hundred Tu-124s, ČSA bought three and it is also used by the Indian Air Force.

In 1967 Aeroflot again introduced two new types of turbine-powered aircraft. The first was the Ilyushin Il-62 which resembles the British VC10 and has four rear-mounted engines and a high T-tail. The only Soviet four-engined jet aircraft in service, the Il-62, is powered by 23,148 lb thrust Kuznetsov NK-8 bypass engines and in standard layout has 168 seats. The Il-62 made its first flight in January 1963 but a number of problems were encountered during the test programme and it did not begin carrying passengers until March 1967. In September 1967 Il-62s began operating Moscow–

Montreal services and in the following month were introduced on services from Moscow to Rome, Paris and Delhi. On 15 July 1968 Il-62s opened the first Soviet services between Moscow and New York. In the previous month these four-jet aircraft had been introduced by Aeroflot on the Moscow–London route. Il-62s are also in service with ČSA, 'LOT', Tarom and Interflug.

The other type introduced by Aeroflot in 1967 was the Tu-134 which is a rear-engined T-tail 72-passenger development of the Tu-124 and thus a direct development of the Tu-104. The Tu-134 was designed to provide economic operation and improved standards of comfort over routes of about 300 to 1,700 nautical miles in length. It is powered by two 14,991 lb thrust Soloviev D-30 turbofans and can operate from rough grass aerodromes.

The Tu-134 entered passenger service on 9 September 1967, between Moscow and Adler/Sochi, and its first international operation was on 12 September 1967 between Moscow and Stockholm. Tu-134s are coming into service in increasing numbers with Aeroflot and are also in service with Aviogenex in Yugoslavia, Balkan, ČSA, Interflug, Malév and Polskie Linie Lotnicze.

Although the An-10s, Il-18s and Tu-104s have given good service to Aeroflot they have all been in use for a considerable time. It therefore became necessary to design a new aircraft to replace them which had increased capacity to cater for the rapidly growing traffic. To meet this requirement the Tupolev design bureau produced the Tu-154. This is a large three-engined aircraft roughly comparable to the Boeing 727-200. It is of similar layout to the Tu-134 but has three rear-mounted engines, one on each side of the fuselage and one inside the fuselage with its air intake on top of the fuselage forward of the fin.

The engines are 20,943 lb thrust Kuznetsov NK-8-2 turbofans and the outer units have thrust reversers for runway braking. The basic Tu-154 has 158 seats but a 164-seat layout can be used and an enlarged 240/250-passenger development is under discussion. The first Tu-154 was completed in August 1968 and made its maiden flight in October 1968. It is likely to become one of Aeroflot's most important aeroplanes.

With the USSR's vast area of more than $8\frac{1}{2}$ mn square miles and its population of about 250 mn, it is obvious that the Aeroflot route network must be served by a fairly wide range of aircraft. Having developed a whole series of jet and propeller-turbine powered airliners for the main domestic and international routes, the Soviet Union was anxious to replace the small single-engined An-2 biplanes and Yak-12 monoplanes which for years have served the short-stage local services. For these short routes two new aircraft were produced, the trijet Yakovlev Yak-40 and the twin propeller-turbine Beriev Be-30.

The Yak-40 is a very neat 24/31-passenger low-wing cantilever monoplane with three rear-mounted 3,306 lb thrust Ivchenko AI-25 turbofans and a T-tail. The wing is unsweptback in order to provide good low-speed handling and the take-off and landing runs are less than 1,200 ft. Yak-40s began regular service in September 1968. The 500th was produced in 1974 and several have been exported to Europe and Afghanistan.

The Be-30 is a high-wing monoplane with retractable undercarriage and two 970 hp TVD-10 propeller-turbines. It has seats for fourteen or fifteen passengers, is designed for stages of up to 430 nautical miles, can take-off with a run of only 557 ft, and is equipped for automatic landing approaches down to 100 ft. The prototype made its first flight in March 1967.

In extreme contrast to the little Be-30 is the Antonov An-22 which has a wing span of 211 ft $3\frac{1}{2}$ in, a loaded weight of 551,160 lb and a payload of 176,370 lb. This is a high-wing monoplane with four 15,000 hp Kuznetsov NK-12 propeller-turbines, twin-fin tail unit, and twelve-wheel main undercarriage. The An-22 was designed to carry bulky loads – its hold measures more than 108 ft in length and nearly $14\frac{1}{2}$ ft in width and height – and yet be able to operate from rough aerodromes. Operated by both Aeroflot and the Soviet Air Force, the An-22 is not known to have been used for passenger carriage and the projected 724-seat variant has been abandoned.

In 1971 the 165-ft span Ilyushin Il-76 freighter made its first flight. This is a high-wing monoplane with four podded turbofans and a payload of 40 tons. Due to fly during 1975 is the 350-passenger Il-86 which is of similar layout to the Boeing 707 and will have four wing-mounted 26,455 lb thrust Soloviev turbofans, nine-abreast seating and lower-deck cargo and baggage holds. Expected to follow about a year behind the Il-86, the 100/120-passenger trijet Yakovlev Yak-42 in fact flew in March 1975.

The Soviet supersonic transport, the Tu-144, is described in Chapter 15.

	Span		Length		Passengers	Loaded weight	Cruising speed	Range
ANT-9	77′	$10\frac{1}{4}''$	55′	$9\frac{1}{4}''$	9	11,111 lb	105·6 mph	621 miles
Il-12	104′	0″	69′	11″	27/32	38,030 lb	217·4 mph	775 miles
Il-14	104′	0″	69′	11″	18/32	38,581 lb	217·4 mph	745 miles
Tu-104A	113′	4″	127′	$5\frac{1}{2}''$	50/115	167,551 lb	497·1 mph	1,925 miles
An-10A	124′	8″	111′	$6\frac{1}{2}''$	100	119,050 lb	391·4 mph	757 miles
Il-18D	122′	$8\frac{1}{2}''$	117′	$9\frac{1}{2}''$	84/122	141,096 lb	388·3 mph	2,485 miles
An-24	95′	$9\frac{1}{2}''$	77′	$2\frac{1}{4}''$	37/50	46,297 lb	310·6 mph	403 miles
Tu-124	83′	10″	100′	4″	44/56	82,673 lb	540·5 mph	775 miles
Il-62	142′	$0\frac{3}{4}''$	174′	$3\frac{1}{4}''$	75/186	347,227 lb	559·2 mph	4,162 miles
Tu-134	95′	$1\frac{3}{4}''$	112′	$8\frac{1}{4}''$	72	103,617 lb	546·8 mph	1,490 miles
Yak-40	82′	$0\frac{1}{4}''$	66′	3″	24/31	28,990 lb	372·8 mph	372 miles
Tu-154	123′	$2\frac{1}{2}''$	157′	$1\frac{3}{4}''$	128/164	189,598 lb	559·2 mph	1,770 miles
Il-86	158′	$6\frac{3}{4}''$	191′	11″	350	414,470 lb	590 mph	3,420 miles

15

Into the Future

The earlier chapters of this book have traced the development of the airliner from the converted single-engined bombers of the First World War to the present when large jet-powered sweptwing monoplanes with seats for up to five hundred passengers are flying the world's air routes at around 600 mph.

Since the introduction of the Boeing 747, described in Chapter 12, three other turbofan-powered widebodied types have gone into regular airline service. They are the McDonnell Douglas DC-10, Lockheed L-1011 TriStar and European A300 Airbus. Each type has large capacity and is much quieter than all the earlier jet transports. By early 1975 more than five hundred wide-bodied airliners had been delivered and these types will carry a high proportion of the passenger and cargo traffic during the remaining years of the century.

The DC-10 and L-1011 are three-engined aeroplanes of very similar appearance. They are lowwing monoplanes with sweptback wings and both have two engines carried in wing-suspended pods and one rear-mounted engine. In the L-1011 the rear engine is inside the fuselage but the DC-10's rear engine is in the base of the vertical fin. Both types have fuselages of about 20 ft in diameter. Various seating layouts can be used but they can carry up to four hundred passengers.

The DC-10 made its first flight on 29 August 1970, the Lockheed TriStar on 16 November 1970 and the Airbus on 28 October 1972.

The standard DC-10 Series 10, powered by 40,000 lb thrust General Electric CF6-6 engines, entered service on 5 August 1971 on American Airlines' Los Angeles–Chicago route, and on 14 August

A white and green Douglas DC-10-30 of Pakistan International Airlines.

that year it was introduced on the San Francisco–Washington route by United Air Lines. The DC-10-10 was followed by two longer range and heavier versions, the Series 30 and 40 (the latter originally being known as the -20). The -30 has 51,000 lb thrust CF6-50 engines, has been built in greater numbers than the other models, and was introduced on Swissair's North Atlantic services on 15 December 1972. The -40 has 49,400 lb thrust Pratt & Whitney JT9D-20 engines, was built for Northwest Airlines and entered service on 16 December 1972. The first convertible passenger/cargo models were delivered in April 1973; by the beginning of 1975 a total of 216 DC-10s had been ordered, 169 had been delivered to more than thirty airlines and options taken on 38 more.

The TriStar entered service on 24 April 1972 with Eastern Air Lines and about 150 had been ordered by the beginning of 1975. All those delivered had 42,000 lb thrust Rolls-Royce RB.211 engines but in September 1974 Saudi Arabian Airlines ordered the first of the heavier and longer range L-1011-200s with 48,000 lb thrust RB-211-524 engines.

A Pacific Southwest Airlines' Lockheed TriStar.

The 192/345-passenger A300B European Airbus is a truly international aeroplane, being produced by Airbus Industrie which comprises Deutsche Airbus, Aérospatiale, Fokker/VFW, CASA of Spain, and Hawker Siddeley which is responsible for the wings. The A300B, although wide-bodied, is smaller than the United States designs and has its two 51,000 lb thrust General Electric CF6-50C turbofans wing mounted. The first version, the A300B-2 entered service with Air France on the Paris–London route on 23 May 1974. The heavier and longer range B-4 model has been ordered by Lufthansa

and there are projects for a bigger B-9, smaller B-10 and a four-engined B-11 with a range of 6,000 miles.

Another recent European airliner is the Dassault-Breguet Mercure which first flew on 28 May 1971 and entered service in 1974 with the French domestic airline Air Inter. The Mercure is a short-range aircraft with 140–159 seats and two wing-mounted 15,500 lb thrust Pratt & Whitney JT8D turbofans. Only the Air Inter order for ten had been placed by the beginning of 1975.

Although the airlines are served mainly by 550–600 mph jets which can fly between New York and

London in 6 hr and Europe and Australia in a little over a day and a night, there are people who believe that progress demands even greater speed and as a result thousands of millions have been spent in pounds, francs, dollars and roubles to build supersonic transports (SSTs) capable of flying at up to more than two and a half times the speed of sound – that is, above Mach 2·5.

When flying at supersonic speed an aircraft structure is subject to very high temperatures which limit the conventional light-alloy aeroplane to about Mach 2·3. To reach the higher speeds steel and titanium have to be used and it is in the choice of materials and size that America has differed from Britain, France and the Soviet Union in designing and building the SST.

Britain and France decided to work together on a fifty–fifty basis to build the Concorde, and Sud-Aviation* and the British Aircraft Corporation were given the responsibility for the airframe and Bristol† and SNECMA joint development of the powerplant. Components are built in England and France without duplication, and transported to Filton, near Bristol, and Toulouse for incorporation on the assembly lines.

The Concorde is a slim delta with finely tapered

* Now Aérospatiale.
† Now Rolls-Royce.

circular-section fuselage and broad fin and rudder. It has neither tailplane nor elevators. The four 38,300 lb thrust Olympus turbojets are carried in pairs beneath the wing and are equipped with reheat, a method for increasing thrust. In production aircraft there will be maximum seating for up to 144 but the fuselage is so narrow that first class seating will be three-across and economy class four-across. For take-off and landing the nose section of the aircraft is drooped to improve the view from the flight deck.

The first Concorde flew from Toulouse on 2 March 1969, and the first Filton-assembled prototype made its first flight on 9 April 1969. The first supersonic flight was made on 1 October 1969, and the aircraft reached Mach 2 for the first time in 1970. Options to buy 74 Concordes had been taken by the beginning of 1970 by sixteen airlines including Air France, BOAC, Air Canada, Air-India, Japan Air Lines, Lufthansa, MEA, Pan American, Qantas and TWA; but the only actual orders by early 1975 were four for Air France and five for British Airways. The Concorde is scheduled to enter service early in 1976.

The first supersonic transport to fly was the Soviet Tupolev Tu-144 which closely resembles the Concorde and has four 28,660 lb thrust NK-144 turbofans. Like the Concorde, the Tu-144 is a slim delta and it, too, has a drooping nose, but its wing is of simpler design and may not be as efficient at low speeds. The Tu-144 made its first flight on 31 December 1968, and its first supersonic flight on 5 June 1969. It is designed to cruise at Mach 2·35 compared with Mach 2·05 for the Concorde.

The United States held a competition for the design of a supersonic transport and chose the Boeing variable-geometry project which was then abandoned in favour of the 745,000 lb 298-passenger Boeing 2707 delta-wing design. Twenty-six airlines secured delivery positions on 122 of them but after a while the entire project was cancelled.

Although the big jets will play a major role during the next decades there is likely to be large-scale growth of short-haul operations. Road, airport and airway congestion can be eased by use of the STOL

(Short Take-Off and Landing) aeroplane which does not require the main runways or jet airways. In 1974 an experimental STOL service was begun between Montreal and Ottawa using Twin Otters and in February 1975 a new STOL airliner left the factory to begin its trials.

The new aeroplane is the de Havilland Canada DHC-7, or Dash 7. It is a 50-passenger high-wing monoplane capable of operating from 2,000 ft runways and powered by four 1,174 hp United Aircraft of Canada PT6A-50 turbines which drive special quiet propellers. Even before the Dash 7 had flown it had been ordered by Air West and Eastern Provincial Airways in Canada, Rocky Mountain Airways of Denver and the Norwegian Widerøe's Flyveselskap. Entry into scheduled service is due early in 1977.

	Span	Length	Passengers	Loaded weight	Cruising speed	Range
BAC/Aérospatiale Concorde	83′ 10″	204′ 0″	128/144	385,000 lb	1,354 mph	5,240 miles
Tupolev Tu-144	81′ 0″	180′ 0″	126	330,000 lb	1,548 mph	4,030 miles
Douglas DC-10-30	165′ 4″	182′ 0″	270/380	555,000 lb	575 mph	6,000 miles
Lockheed L-1011 TriStar	170′ 0″	182′ 8″	272/400	575,000 lb	575 mph	4,606 miles
Airbus A300B-4	147′ 1¼″	175′ 11″	192/345	330,700 lb	580 mph	3,900 miles
de Havilland Canada Dash 7	93′ 0″	80′ 4″	50	41,000 lb	275 mph	885 miles

FURTHER READING

Airlines of the United States since 1914, R. E. G. Davies, Putnam, 1972

Airspeed Aircraft since 1931, H. A. Taylor, Putnam, 1970

Annals of British and Commonwealth Air Transport 1919–60, John Stroud, Putnam, 1962

Avro Aircraft since 1908, A. J. Jackson, Putnam, 1965

Boeing Aircraft since 1916, P. M. Bowers, Putnam, 1966

Bristol Aircraft since 1910, C. H. Barnes, Putnam, 1964

British Aviation: The Great War and Armistice, Harald J. Penrose, Putnam, 1969

British Civil Aircraft 1919–59, A. J. Jackson, Putnam, 1959

Civil Airliners since 1946, Kenneth Munson, Blandford Press, 1967

De Havilland Aircraft since 1915, A. J. Jackson, Putnam, 1962

D.H. An Outline of De Havilland History, C. Martin Sharp, Faber and Faber, 1960

European Transport Aircraft since 1910, John Stroud, Putnam, 1966

Fokker – The Man and the Aircraft, Henri Hegener, Harleyford Publications, 1961

Ford Story, The, A Pictorial History of the Ford Tri-motor 1927–1957, William T. Larkins, The Robert R. Longo Co Inc, USA, 1957

Handbook of the Vickers Viscount, P. St John Turner, Ian Allan, 1968

Handley Page, Donald C. Clayton, Ian Allan, 1970

Modern Airliner, The, Peter W. Brooks, Putnam, 1961

Shorts Aircraft since 1900, C. H. Barnes, Putnam, 1967

Soviet Transport Aircraft since 1945, John Stroud, Putnam, 1968

Tin Goose, Douglas J. Ingells, Aero Publishers, USA

Turbine-engined Airliners of the World, F. G. Swanborough, Temple Press, 1962

Vickers Aircraft since 1908, C. F. Andrews, Putnam, 1969

INDEX OF PRINCIPAL AIRCRAFT